Vegetarian Cookbook

Simple & Quick

The 150 tastiest recipes

Oksana Verova

Foreword

In this book, you will find a selection of 150 vegetarian dishes.

When I put them together, I always avoid exotic ingredients. The recipes are also kept simple. So there are no excuses not to try vegetarian.

I hope you enjoy this selection of quick and easy recipes.

Enjoy your meal!

Table of contents

Foreword..2
Advance - Information...8
Advantages of a vegetarian diet..9
Starters, salads and breakfast...10
　　Carrot salad..11
　　Egg salad..12
　　Tomato salad..13
　　Bulgur salad...14
　　Broccoli salad...15
　　Beetroot salad..16
　　Potato salad...17
　　Rice pudding..18
　　French toast...19
　　Armer Knight...20
　　Garlic bread...21
　　Cheese omelette...22
　　Bruschetta...23
　　Porridge...24
　　Scrambled eggs with tomatoes...25
Soups..26
　　Potato soup..27
　　Vegetable soup...28
　　Cream of pumpkin soup...29
　　Tomato soup..30
　　Lentil soup...31
　　Gazpacho (cold soup)..32
　　Red Lentil Coconut Soup...34
　　Broccoli cream soup...35
　　Cauliflower soup..36
　　Buckwheat - paprika soup..37
　　Barley soup..38
　　Cream of asparagus soup...39
　　Cream of mushroom soup..40

Minestrone..41
Savoy cabbage soup...42
Rice soup..43
Pea soup...44
Onion soup...45
Kale soup..46
Spinach soup..47
Coconut soup...48
Nettle soup...49
Cream of garlic soup...50
Cheese leek soup..51
Sweet potato soup..52
Green spelt soup..53
Chestnut soup..54
Turnip soup..55
Hot & Sour Soup...56
Dhal soup...58
Carrot soup..60
Main courses...61
Vegetable - coconut stew..62
Kohlrabi vegetables...63
Borscht...64
Falafel...66
Potato dumplings...67
Soy Schnitzel "Viennese Style".................................68
Asian Tempeh Pan...69
Thai curry..70
Chop Suey..72
Chakalaka" vegetable stew..74
Potato gratin..75
Tofu dish "Bibimbap...76
Asian vegetables with smoked tofu..........................78
Pad Thai" rice noodle dish.......................................80
Tomato-Lentil Stew...82
Mincemeat stew...84

Ratatouille...85
Spaghetti Carbonara...86
Spaghetti Napoli..88
Potato goulash...90
Paella..92
Mushroom - noodle pan.....................................94
Pizza...95
Stuffed mushrooms...96
Smoked Tofu Casserole......................................97
Oven vegetables...98
Spinach - Risotto...99
Sweet potato casserole.....................................100
Pumpkin ragout...101
Kidney Beans - Stew..102
Nasi Goreng..104
White bean stew...106
Chili sin Carne...108
Tofu noodles...110
Vegetables - Sushi...112
Spaghetti with peanut sauce...........................114
Coconut spaghetti...115
Baked Beans..116
Pichelsteiner...117
Spiced rice...118
Tofu - Gyros...119
Chickpea curry...120
Potato - Carrot Rösti..121
Paprika - Couscous...122
Grilled Pepper skewers.....................................123
Grilled Mushroom Skewers.............................124
Grilled corn on the cob....................................125
Sauces, dips, dressings and spreads...............126
Guacamole...127
Raspberry dressing..128
Muhammara..129

Sate sauce...130
Pineapple curry sauce...132
Peanut butter...133
Hummus..134
Coconut spread...135
Paprika chickpea spread..136
Strawberry cream cheese spread..............................137
Onion lard..138
Hazelnut - Chocolate Cream....................................139
Tomato spread..140
Mushroom spread...141
Obatzter...142
Vegetarian liver sausage..143
Hungarian style paprika sauce.................................144
Aioli...145
Pizza spread..146
Tzatziki..147
Spaghetti sauce "Aglio Olio....................................148
Pesto..149
Lentil spread...150
Blueberry sauce..152
Desserts and sweets...153
Crêpes..154
Chocolate ice cream..155
Waffles...156
Sweet couscous...157
Lemon - Donuts..158
Pancake..160
Apple-almond porridge..161
Chia pudding..162
Pancakes..163
Baked banana...164
Banana cookies...165
Brownies..166
Schokocrossies..167

Chocolate muffins..168
Popcorn with caramel sauce....................................169
Dulce de leche" dessert..170
Chocolate mousse...171
Strawberry - Tiramisu in a glass............................172
Roasted almonds..173
Chocolate cake...174
Apple tart...175
Strawberry sorbet...176
Red wine cake..177
Drinks and smoothies...178
Banana milkshake...179
Golden milk..180
Mulled wine..181
Children's punch...182
Lemonade...183
Strawberry Yoghurt Smoothie.................................184
Raspberry Smoothie..185
Green smoothie...186
Pineapple Smoothie...187
Strawberry Banana Smoothie..................................188
Watermelon Smoothie...189
Kiwi Banana Smoothie..190
Disclaimer...191
Imprint..192

Advance - Information

The baking times given are from my oven. Please note that there can often be deviations.

If you use top/bottom heat, raise the temperature by 20 degrees C.

All recipes can be modified according to your own wishes.

Vegetables should always be bought of organic quality.

Always wash the vegetables. I did not specify this in the recipes.

A fresh spice can also be used instead of powder.

Instead of one cube of yeast, 2 packets of dry yeast can be used.

Xylith can also be used instead of sugar.

Abbreviations

TK = Frozen

TL = teaspoon

EL= tablespoon

Advantages of a vegetarian diet

A vegetarian diet is a diet that excludes meat and fish but includes eggs and dairy products.

<u>Some benefits of a vegetarian diet are:</u>

- Better health: Vegetarians suffer less often from heart disease, high blood pressure, and diabetes than meat-eaters.

- Less environmental impact: The production of animal products can be extremely harmful to the environment due to the consumption of fossil fuels and other resources.

- More humane: Eating meat can lead to animal cruelty, as animals on farms are often treated inhumanely.

Starters, salads and breakfast

Carrot salad

Ingredients (4 servings)

1 kg carrots

1 onion

1 clove of garlic

100 ml (rapeseed) oil

1 tablespoon vinegar

1 tsp salt

1 tsp coriander

1 tsp sugar

Preparation

Grate the carrots and mix with vinegar.

Press the garlic clove and dice the onion.

Heat the oil in a pot.

Add the onion and garlic and fry for 3 minutes over medium heat.

Pour the contents of the pot over the carrots and mix with the remaining ingredients.

Leave to stand for 15 minutes before serving.

Egg salad

Ingredients (4 servings)

8 eggs

2 tablespoons mayonnaise

1 pinch of salt

1 pinch of pepper

1 tablespoon vinegar

2 tbsp sour cream

1 tsp mustard

Chives for garnish.

It seems that there is a pronoun problem here.

Preparation

Hard-boil the eggs in a pot of water for 10 minutes.

Quench the eggs with cold water, peel and cut them into small pieces.

Mix the mayonnaise, vinegar, salt, pepper, mustard and sour cream in a bowl.

Mix in the eggs and leave them in the fridge for 2 hours.

Before serving, season again with salt and pepper and garnish with chives.

Tomato salad

Ingredients (4 servings)

500 g tomatoes

3 tablespoons balsamic vinegar

1 bunch parsley or chives

Salt and pepper

Preparation

Quarter the tomatoes. Finely chop the parsley or chop the chives.

Put the tomatoes in a bowl and drizzle with balsamic vinegar.

Season to taste with salt and pepper.

Garnish with parsley or chives.

Bulgur salad

Ingredients (4 servings)

300 g bulgur

1 bunch of spring onions, cut into rings

300 ml tomato juice

300 ml water

3 tablespoons parsley

4 tbsp peanuts

1 pinch cinnamon

7 tbsp (rapeseed) oil

Salt and pepper

Preparation

Heat the oil in a pan and sauté the spring onion.
Add the bulgur and sauté for 2 minutes over medium heat.
Add water, tomato juice, salt and pepper.
Simmer the bulgur for 10 minutes, covered, over low heat.
Roast the peanuts in a pan.
Sprinkle with cinnamon and roast.
Mix the parsley and peanuts into the bulgur and serve hot.

Broccoli salad

Ingredients (4 servings)

250 g broccoli - florets

1 red pepper

1 Apple

30 g pine nuts

2 tsp mustard

2 tsp honey

2 tbsp olive oil

1 tablespoon balsamic vinegar

Salt and pepper

Preparation

Cut the broccoli, peppers and apple into very small pieces and place them in a bowl with the pine nuts.

Mix the remaining ingredients to make a marinade.

Mix the contents of the bowl well with the marinade.

Leave to infuse for 5 minutes and then serve.

Beetroot salad

Ingredients (4 servings)

1 package beetroot, cooked and peeled

1 handful of walnuts

1 handful of dried plums

1 clove of garlic

1 tsp salt

1 tsp sugar

Preparation

Press the garlic clove and grate the beetroot.

Mix all the ingredients together.

Leave to infuse in the fridge for at least 2 hours.

Potato salad

Ingredients (4 people)

1 kg potatoes

1 onion

80 ml vinegar

1 tsp salt

1 tsp pepper

Preparation

Boil potatoes.

Peel the potatoes and cut them into slices.

Finely dice the onion.

Mix all the ingredients together and leave to infuse for a while.

The salad can be enjoyed warm or cold.

Rice pudding

Ingredients (4 servings)

1000 ml milk

250 g rice pudding

30 g sugar

1 sachet of vanilla sugar

For sprinkling: Cinnamon

Preparation

Bring the milk to boil in a saucepan.

Add the rice, sugar and vanilla sugar and leave to swell for 30 minutes with the lid on low.

Stir frequently so that nothing burns.

When the rice has reached the desired doneness, remove it from the heat.

Divide onto plates and sprinkle with cinnamon.

French toast

Ingredients

1 half banana

200 ml milk

40 g flour

1 pinch cinnamon

1 tsp parmesan

½ tsp baking powder

4 slices of toast

1 tbsp redcurrant jam

200 ml (rapeseed) oil

½ tbsp icing sugar (for sprinkling)

Preparation

Put the milk, Parmesan, flour, cinnamon and baking powder in a deep dish.

Mash half a peeled banana and let it sit with the breadcrumb mixture for 5 minutes.

Spread two slices of toast with jam and top with the other two slices.

Heat a pan with about one centimetre of oil in it.

Pull the toast through the breadcrumb mixture on both sides and fry for 5 minutes on both sides over medium heat until golden brown.

Drain the toast slices on kitchen paper and sprinkle with icing sugar.

Divide onto plates and sprinkle with cinnamon.

Armer Knight

Ingredients

4 - 5 slices of toast

1 ripe banana

200 ml milk

3 tablespoons sugar

1 tbsp flour

2 pinches cinnamon

1 sachet of vanilla sugar

1 tbsp butter for frying

Preparation

Mash the banana in a bowl with a fork.

Add the milk, flour, vanilla sugar, and cinnamon and mix well.

Cut the toast slices in half and soak them in the banana milk until they are soaked.

Heat the butter in a frying pan and fry the toast slices on both sides over medium heat.

Serve sprinkled with sugar.

Garlic bread

Ingredients

300 g (black) bread

2 garlic cloves

3 pinches salt

1 pinch of sugar

5 tsp (rapeseed) oil

Preparation

Cut the bread into small strips.

Heat the oil in a pan.

Fry the bread in it until crispy on all sides.

In a bowl, mix bread with salt and sugar.

Squeeze the garlic cloves and mix them into the bread.

The bread can be eaten warm or cold as a snack.

Cheese omelette

Ingredients (4 servings)

12 eggs

100 g mountain cheese

2 tbsp (rapeseed) oil

2 tablespoons butter

Salt and pepper

Preparation

Grate the cheese.

Season the eggs with salt and pepper in a bowl and whisk with a fork.

Heat the butter and oil in a pan and add the eggs.

Sauté over medium heat for 3 minutes.

Sprinkle the cheese over the egg mixture and allow it to melt.

Fold the omelette in half and fry for 2 minutes.

Bruschetta

Ingredients (2 servings)

4 slices of white bread or toast

2 diced tomatoes

Some olive oil

Preparation

Toast the bread slices with 1 tbsp olive oil in a pan until crisp. Top generously with the diced tomatoes.

Drizzle with olive oil and serve on a plate.

Porridge

Ingredients (2 servings)

100 g seeded oat flakes

400 g water

about 100 g milk

1 banana

2 tablespoons flaked almonds

1 tbsp sultanas (optional)

2 tablespoons sugar

Preparation

Cut the banana into small pieces.

Bring the water, salt, and sultanas to the boil in a saucepan.

Stir in the oat flakes and simmer gently on low heat for 5 minutes, stirring constantly.

When the mixture thickens slightly, mix in the banana pieces well.

Serve in a deep dish and sprinkle with sugar.

Sprinkle the flaked almonds over the top and add the desired amount of milk.

Scrambled eggs with tomatoes

Ingredients

4 eggs

1 tsp vegetable stock powder

1 tbsp paprika powder, chilli

1 clove of garlic

2 onions

2 tbsp (rapeseed) oil

3-4 tomatoes

Preparation

Cut the onions into thin rings and press the garlic clove.

Heat the oil in a pan and brown the onion.

Mix together the eggs, vegetable stock powder, garlic, and paprika powder in a bowl.

Add the contents of the bowl to the onions in the pan.

Fry, occasionally stirring, until the eggs begin to set and take on a scrambled egg consistency.

Chop the tomatoes and serve with scrambled eggs.

Soups

Potato soup

Ingredients (4 people)

600 g potatoes

1000 ml vegetable stock

150 g leek, cut into rings

3 carrots, sliced

1 onion, diced

1 clove of garlic, pressed

1 tbsp (rapeseed) oil

1 tablespoon parsley

2 tablespoons marjoram

Salt and pepper (to taste)

Preparation

Heat a saucepan with oil and gently fry the vegetables, except the potatoes, for 5 minutes, stirring occasionally.

Add the marjoram and the potatoes to the pot.

Deglaze with the vegetable stock and season with salt and pepper.

Put the lid on and boil for 15 minutes until the potatoes are cooked.

Add the parsley and season with salt and pepper.

Blend coarsely with a hand blender.

Vegetable soup

Ingredients (4 people)

100 g short hollow noodles

1000 ml vegetable stock

1 can of chopped tomatoes

100 g green beans, cut 1 cm long

100 g savoy cabbage, cut into fine strips

1 carrot, diced

1 onion, finely chopped

1 courgette, diced

2 tbsp tomato paste

Salt and pepper (to taste)

2 tbsp (rapeseed) oil

Preparation

Heat the oil in a pot and sauté the onion in it.

Add the savoy cabbage and green beans and sauté briefly.

Stir in tomato paste and deglaze with vegetable stock and chopped tomatoes.

Add the pasta and simmer for 10 minutes, stirring from time to time.

Add the courgettes and simmer for another 5 minutes.

Season to taste with salt and pepper.

Cream of pumpkin soup

Ingredients

500 g Hokkaido pumpkin, seeded and cut into small cubes

600 ml vegetable soup

150 ml cream

1 onion, finely diced

1 clove of garlic, pressed

½ tsp ginger powder

1 pinch nutmeg

2 pinches pepper

3 tbsp (rapeseed) oil for frying

Pumpkin seed oil for drizzling

Preparation

Sauté the garlic clove and onion in a pot with oil until translucent.

Add the pumpkin and fry briefly.

Pour in the vegetable soup.

Add the spices and simmer for 20 minutes.

When the pumpkin is soft, add the cream and purée the soup.

If the soup is too thick, add a little water and bring it to the boil.

Serve the soup on a plate and drizzle with pumpkin seed oil.

Tomato soup

Ingredients (4 people)

400g chopped tomatoes (or fresh, of course)

1 onion, finely chopped

1 clove of garlic, pressed

2 pinches chilli

½ bunch basil

250 ml vegetable stock

2 pinches pepper

125 g Tuscan white bread (preferably from the day before)

2 tbsp olive oil

Preparation

Cut the white bread into small cubes.

Heat the oil in a pot and sauté the onion and garlic until translucent.

Add the tomatoes, chilli, salt, and pepper with the vegetable stock and bring to the boil.

Simmer for 15 minutes on medium heat.

Add the white bread cubes and basil and simmer for another 10 minutes on medium heat.

Stir the soup through and remove it from the heat.

Leave to infuse for 10 minutes and heat again before eating.

Serve on deep plates drizzled with olive oil.

Lentil soup

Ingredients (4 people)

1000 g water

250 g red lentils

1 potato

2 carrots

1 onion

1 tablespoon butter

1 tsp lemon juice

3 pinches pepper

Preparation

Wash the lentils well.

Peel the potato, onion and carrot and cut them into small pieces.

Then put these ingredients in a pot with water and bring to the boil.

Simmer for 20 minutes.

Puree the soup with a hand blender.

Add the remaining ingredients and bring the soup to the boil again briefly.

Serve hot.

Gazpacho (cold soup)

Ingredients

850 ml tomato juice

1 onion

½ medium cucumber

½ green pepper

½ red pepper

3 tomatoes

2 garlic cloves

6 slices of white bread

6 tbsp olive oil

3 tbsp white wine vinegar

½ tsp sugar

1 tsp salt

1 tsp pepper

Preparation

Squeeze the garlic cloves and set them aside separately.

Finely chop the vegetables and place them in a bowl with garlic cloves.

Add the tomato juice, vinegar, oil, sugar, salt and pepper and mix well.

Puree the vegetable soup with a blender and refrigerate.

Preheat the oven to 180 degrees C.

Cut the white bread into 1 cm cubes.

Mix the oil with the second clove of garlic and pour over the diced white bread.

Place the white bread on a baking tray lined with baking paper and bake for 10 minutes until golden brown. Stir occasionally.

Pour the cold vegetable soup into deep plates and sprinkle with the white bread cubes.

Red Lentil Coconut Soup

Ingredients (4 people)
400 ml coconut milk

700 ml vegetable stock

180 g red lentils, washed and drained

1 onion, diced

1 clove of garlic, pressed

1 carrot, sliced

2 tsp curry powder

2 tablespoons lemon juice

2 pinches pepper

some (rapeseed) oil for frying

Preparation

Heat the oil in a pot and sauté the onion, garlic, and curry powder for about 1 minute.

Add the lentils and carrot and steam briefly.

Deglaze with the vegetable stock and add the coconut milk. Then bring to the boil.

Simmer gently for 25 minutes until the lentils break down and the vegetables are soft.

Now puree the soup and finely strain through a sieve.

Finally, season the soup with lemon juice and pepper.

Broccoli cream soup

Ingredients (4 people)

1 broccoli

4 potatoes

1 onion

1 clove of garlic

800 ml vegetable stock

200 ml coconut milk

2 tbsp (rapeseed) oil

Salt to taste

Preparation

Dice the potatoes, chop the onion and press the garlic clove.

Heat a pot with oil and fry the onion until translucent.

Add the vegetable stock, garlic, and potatoes and cook in the closed pot for 10 minutes.

Meanwhile, cut off the broccoli florets and chop the stems.

Add the broccoli and coconut milk and cook for another 15 minutes.

Season with salt and bring to the boil again briefly.

Cauliflower soup

Ingredients (4 people)

1 cauliflower, in small pieces

1 potato, in small cubes

3 carrots, thinly sliced

2 onions, finely chopped

1 clove of garlic, pressed

700 ml vegetable stock

1 tsp curry powder

½ tsp ginger powder

2 pinches pepper

3 tbsp (rapeseed) oil

1 tbsp parsley to garnish

Preparation

Heat the oil in a pot and sauté the onion and garlic until translucent.

Add the cauliflower and carrots and sauté briefly.

Deglaze with the vegetable stock, add the spices and simmer for 20 minutes.

Puree the soup with a hand blender.

If the soup is too thick, add a little water and bring it to the boil.

Serve the soup on a plate and garnish with parsley.

Buckwheat - paprika soup

Ingredients (4 people)

100 g buckwheat

300 g potatoes

1 (red) pepper

1 Carrot

1 onion

1000 ml warm vegetable stock

250 ml cream

2 tbsp (rapeseed) oil

Salt to taste.

Preparation

Peel and wash the potatoes and cut them into small pieces.

Finely chop the onion and cut the pepper and carrot into small pieces.

Heat the oil in a high pan and fry the onion, pepper and carrot for 3 minutes.

Add the vegetable stock, buckwheat and potato and simmer for 30 minutes over medium heat.

Add the cream and simmer for another 10 minutes.

Season with salt and serve on deep plates.

Barley soup

Ingredients (4 people)

150 g pearl barley (medium)

125 g smoked tofu, diced

5 potatoes, diced

1 small piece of celery, diced

2 carrots

1 onion, finely chopped

½ stick leek, cut into rings

1500 ml vegetable stock

3 tbsp. soy sauce

1 pinch nutmeg

2 pinches pepper

2 tbsp (rapeseed) oil

Parsley to garnish

Preparation

Heat the oil in a pot and sauté the onion until translucent.

Add the pearl barley and sauté until translucent.

Add the rest of the vegetables and fry briefly.

Add the vegetable stock, bring to the boil and simmer gently for 30 minutes until the pearl barley is cooked.

Sear the tofu in a frying pan and add to the pot.

Add the spices, bring to the boil and leave to infuse for 5 minutes.

Serve on deep plates sprinkled with parsley.

Cream of asparagus soup

Ingredients (4 people)

250 g white asparagus, peeled into 3-4 cm pieces

900 ml water (asparagus water and stock)

100 ml cream

40 g flour

1 stock cube

1 tsp lemon juice

1 tsp sugar

1 pinch nutmeg

2 tbsp (rapeseed) oil

Salt to taste - Optional: 2 tbsp white wine

Preparation

Bring the water to the boil in the pot, salt lightly, and cook the asparagus.

Drain the asparagus and collect the asparagus water.

Measure out the asparagus water and, if necessary, top up with water to make 900 ml.

Heat the oil in a saucepan, add the flour, and sweat until light yellow, stirring constantly.

Add the liquid and stock cube (optionally white wine), bring to the boil and turn off the heat. Add the cream and let the soup simmer for 5 minutes. Add the asparagus, sugar, nutmeg, and lemon juice.

The soup can now be pureed to taste.

Season with salt and pepper and serve on deep plates.

Cream of mushroom soup

Ingredients (4 people)

100 g mushrooms, sliced

400 ml water

20 ml cream

1 vegetable stock cube

1 onion, diced

1 clove of garlic, diced

some (rapeseed) oil for sautéing

3 tbsp. flour

½ tsp parsley

1 pinch nutmeg

1 pinch of pepper

some parsley to garnish

Preparation

Heat the oil in a pot and sauté the onion with the garlic clove.

Add the mushrooms and sauté.

Now sweat the flour in the pot.

Add the vegetable stock cube and the water.

Simmer the soup for 10 minutes, stirring constantly.

Then puree and refine with pepper and nutmeg.

Finally, add the cream and sprinkle with parsley.

Minestrone

Ingredients (4 people)

1000 ml vegetable stock

700 g vegetables of choice (e.g., potato, carrot, tomato, etc.)

1 onion

1 tsp salt

3 tbsp (olive) oil for frying

120 g small Italian durum wheat pasta

To serve:

6 tsp olive oil

Optional basil leaves

Preparation

Chop the onion and vegetables.

Heat the oil in a saucepan and fry the onion until translucent.

Add the vegetable stock and vegetables.

Bring to the boil and simmer the soup over low heat for 15 minutes.

Add the salt and noodles.

Cook for the time indicated on the pasta package.

Pour the minestrone into deep plates, drizzle with oil and (optional) garnish with a basil leaf.

Savoy cabbage soup

Ingredients (4 people)

½ whirling head

1 potato

1 carrot

1 onion

1000 ml hot vegetable stock

2 tbsp (rapeseed) oil

50 ml cream

Salt and pepper to taste.

Preparation

Chop the onion, dice the potato and carrot, and cut the savoy cabbage into strips.

Heat the oil in a pot and sauté the onion until translucent.

Add the savoy cabbage and steam briefly.

Add the vegetable stock with the carrot and potato and simmer for 45 minutes.

Add the cream and leave to infuse for 5 minutes.

Season to taste and serve on deep plates.

Rice soup

Ingredients (4 people)

200 g rice

1 carrot

1 bunch chives

1000 ml warm vegetable stock

1 tsp curry

2 tbsp (rapeseed) oil

Salt and pepper to taste

Preparation

Rinse the rice well and drain. Grate the carrot into small pieces.

Heat the oil in a saucepan and sauté the rice until translucent.

Add the vegetable stock, bring to the boil and simmer gently for 20 minutes.

Add the carrot and bring it to the boil briefly.

Add the curry and simmer for 20 minutes.

Chop the chives and add them to the soup.

Season to taste and serve in deep plates.

Pea soup

Ingredients (4 people)

250 g peas

3 potatoes

1 carrot

1 clove of garlic

1 onion

1000 ml vegetable stock

1 tablespoon lovage

2 tsp coriander

1 tsp thyme

1 tsp marjoram

2 tbsp (rapeseed) oil

Salt and pepper to taste

Preparation

Soak the peas overnight for at least 12 hours.

Finely chop the onion and garlic clove.

Finely dice the potatoes and carrots.

Heat the oil in a pot and sauté the onion and garlic until translucent.

Add the vegetable stock, potato, carrot, spices and peas, bring to the boil and simmer gently for 30 minutes.

The soup tastes best when it is left to infuse for 24 hours and then boiled up again.

Season to taste and serve in deep plates.

Onion soup

Ingredients (4 people)

400 g onions

500 ml warm vegetable stock

2 tsp curry

2 tsp coriander

1 tsp caraway

Juice of one lemon

2 tbsp (coconut) oil

Salt and pepper to taste.

Preparation

Chop the onion finely.

Heat the coconut oil in a saucepan and sauté the onion until translucent.

Add the vegetable stock, bring to the boil and simmer gently for 20 minutes.

Add the remaining ingredients and leave to infuse for 5 minutes.

Season to taste and serve in deep plates.

Kale soup

Ingredients (4 people)

300 g kale

2 potatoes

½ jar chickpeas

1 onion

700 ml warm vegetable stock

100 ml cream

2 tbsp (coconut) oil

2 pinches nutmeg

Salt and pepper to taste

Preparation

Chop the onion, dice the potato and shred the kale.

Heat the oil in a pot and sauté the onion until translucent.

Add the potatoes and sauté for 5 minutes, stirring constantly.

Fold in the kale and mix well.

Add the vegetable stock, bring to the boil and simmer gently for 10 minutes, stirring occasionally.

Add the chickpeas and nutmeg and simmer for another 10 minutes.

When the potatoes are firm to the bite, puree the soup with a blender.

Add the cream, bring to the boil briefly and leave to infuse for 5 minutes.

Season with salt and pepper and serve in deep plates.

Spinach soup

Ingredients (4 people)

500 g spinach (fresh or drained frozen spinach)

3 garlic cloves

1000 ml hot vegetable stock

100 ml cream

1 tsp paprika powder

2 tbsp flour

3 tbsp (rapeseed) oil

Salt and pepper to taste

Preparation

Wash the spinach thoroughly, drain well and chop in a blender.

Chop the garlic cloves finely.

Heat the oil in a saucepan and briefly stir in the flour and sauté.

Add the spinach and continue to stir.

Add the vegetable stock and garlic and simmer for 20 minutes.

Add the cream and bring to the boil briefly.

Leave to infuse for 5 minutes.

Season to taste and serve in deep plates.

Coconut soup

Ingredients (4 people)

1 can of coconut milk

300 g potatoes

100 g red lentils

2 carrots

1 onion

2 garlic cloves

600 ml warm vegetable stock

2 tbsp curry powder

2 tablespoons coconut oil

Salt and pepper to taste

Preparation

Wash the lentils and drain.

Finely chop the onion and garlic cloves.

Dice the potatoes and carrots.

Heat the coconut oil in a pot and sauté the onion and garlic.

Add the vegetable stock, potatoes, carrots and lentils, bring to the boil and simmer for 20 minutes.

Puree the soup with a hand blender.

Add the coconut milk and curry powder and bring to boil again.

Leave to infuse for 5 minutes.

Season to taste and serve in deep plates.

Nettle soup

Ingredients (4 people)

500 g nettle leaves

1 potato

1 onion

1000 ml vegetable stock

50 g cream

2 tbsp (rapeseed) oil

Salt and pepper to taste.

1 tbsp chopped chives to garnish

Preparation

Chop the onion, wash the nettle leaves and dice the potato.

Heat the oil in a pot and sauté the onion until translucent.

Add the potato and simmer for another 5 minutes.

Add the nettle leaves and cook for one minute.

Add the vegetable stock and simmer on a low heat for 10 minutes.

Add the cream, bring to the boil and simmer gently for another 5 minutes.

Puree the soup with a hand blender.

Season to taste and sprinkle with chives.

Cream of garlic soup

Ingredients (4 people)

6 garlic cloves

1000 ml warm vegetable stock

4 slices of toast

250 ml cream

2 tablespoons parsley

1 tsp salt

Preparation

Finely chop the garlic cloves.

Dice the toast.

Bring the vegetable stock to boil in the pot, add the garlic and salt.

Simmer for 5 minutes.

Add the toast and simmer for another 10 minutes.

Add the cream and puree the soup with a hand blender.

Leave to infuse for 5 minutes.

Sprinkle with parsley and serve in deep plates.

Cheese leek soup

Ingredients (4 people)

2 leeks

750 ml vegetable stock

1 package of cream cheese

50 g grated cheese (e.g., Gouda)

2 garlic cloves

1 tsp medium-hot mustard

1 onion

1/2 tsp thyme

2 tbsp (rapeseed) oil

1/2 tsp pepper

Preparation

Chop the onion, cut the leek into fine rings and press the garlic.

Heat the oil in a saucepan and fry the onions until golden brown.

Add the garlic and leek and let it steam a little.

Deglaze with the vegetable stock and add the processed cheese, stirring until it has completely dissolved.

Stir in the pepper and mustard.

Sprinkle the soup with cheese and serve.

Sweet potato soup

Ingredients (4 people)

3 sweet potatoes

1 onion

1 clove of garlic

2 tbsp peanut butter

1000 ml hot vegetable stock

1 can of coconut milk

2 tablespoons lemon juice

2 tbsp (rapeseed) oil

Salt and pepper to taste.

Preparation

Finely chop the onion and garlic clove. Dice the sweet potato.

Heat the oil in a pot and sauté the onion and garlic.

Add the vegetable stock and sweet potatoes and simmer for 20 minutes until the sweet potatoes are soft.

Puree the soup with a hand blender.

Stir in the coconut milk, peanut butter and lemon juice.

Season to taste and serve in deep plates.

Green spelt soup

Ingredients (4 people)

90 g green spelt meal

3 Peppers

1 onion

1 clove of garlic

900 ml vegetable stock

50 ml cream

2 tbsp (rapeseed) oil

Salt and pepper to taste

2 tablespoons parsley

Preparation

Clean and roughly dice the peppers, finely dice the onion and press the garlic clove.

Heat a pot with oil and fry the onion until translucent.

Add the green spelt and fry for 3 minutes, stirring constantly.

Deglaze with the vegetable stock and simmer on low heat for 10 minutes.

Add the diced peppers and garlic and simmer gently for another 10 minutes.

Puree the soup.

Add the cream, bring to the boil and leave to infuse for 5 minutes.

Season to taste with salt and pepper.

Serve the soup on deep plates, sprinkled with parsley.

Chestnut soup

Ingredients (4 people)

250 g chestnut puree

1 onion

300 ml vegetable stock

250 ml cream

2 tbsp (rapeseed) oil

Salt and pepper to taste.

Preparation

Finely chop the onion.

Heat the oil in a pot and fry the onion until translucent.

Add the vegetable stock and stir in the chestnut puree.

Simmer the soup for about 15 minutes.

Add the cream and leave to infuse for 5 minutes.

Season with salt and pepper and serve in deep plates.

Turnip soup

Ingredients (4 people)

½ rutabaga, diced small

1 onion, finely diced

1000 ml (cold) vegetable stock

250 ml cream

3 tablespoons butter

2 tbsp flour

½ tsp nutmeg

4 tbsp parmesan

Salt and pepper to taste

Parsley to garnish

Preparation

Heat the butter in a saucepan and sauté the vegetables well.

Dust with flour and prepare a roux.

Add the vegetable stock and bring to the boil.

Simmer on medium heat for 15 minutes.

Puree the soup with a hand blender until creamy.

Add the cream and nutmeg and bring to the boil again.

Simmer on medium heat for 3 minutes.

Stir in the Parmesan and season with salt and pepper.

Serve the soup garnished with parsley.

Hot & Sour Soup

Ingredients (4 people)

200 g smoked tofu

200 g brown mushrooms

1000 ml vegetable stock

140 g bamboo strips (drained from the jar)

½ bunch of spring onions

2 garlic cloves

3 tbsp rice wine vinegar

3 tbsp. soy sauce

3 pinches of chilli powder

2 pinches pepper

1 tsp ginger

3 tbsp starch, dissolved in cold water

1 tablespoon sugar

2 tbsp (rapeseed) oil for frying

Preparation

Press the garlic clove, slice the mushrooms and spring onions.

Dry the tofu and cut it into strips.

Heat the oil in a saucepan and fry the tofu and mushrooms.

Stir in the spring onions, garlic and bamboo.

Deglaze with the vegetable stock and bring to the boil.

Add the remaining ingredients, except the starch, and simmer for 10 minutes over medium heat.

Stir in the dissolved starch and bring the soup to boil again.

When the soup thickens, remove it from the heat and serve on deep plates.

Dhal soup

Ingredients (4 people)

2 small tins of chopped tomatoes

200 g red lentils

750 ml vegetable stock

400 ml coconut milk

1 onion

2 garlic cloves

1 tsp turmeric

1 tsp garam masala

2 pinches of chilli powder

1 tsp cumin

2 tsp lemon juice

1 tablespoon sugar

Salt and chilli powder to taste

2 tbsp (coconut) oil for frying

Preparation

Wash the lentils and drain.

Chop the onion and press the garlic.

Heat the oil in a large pot and sauté the onion and garlic until translucent.

Add the turmeric, garam masala, chilli powder and cumin and fry briefly.

Add the vegetable stock, coconut milk, lentils, and tomatoes and bring to the boil.

Simmer, occasionally stirring, on medium heat for 15 minutes until the lentils are soft.

Add sugar and lemon juice and season with chilli powder and salt.

Carrot soup

Ingredients (4 people)

500 g carrots

1 onion

1 clove of garlic

1000 ml warm vegetable stock

150 ml cream

2 tbsp (rapeseed) oil

1 tsp paprika powder

Salt and pepper to taste.

Preparation

Peel and wash the carrots and cut them into small pieces.

Finely chop the onion and press the garlic clove.

Heat the oil in a high pan and fry the onion and garlic for 3 minutes.

Add the vegetable stock and carrots and simmer until the carrots are soft.

Puree the soup with a hand blender.

Add the cream and paprika powder and leave to infuse for 5 minutes.

Season with salt and pepper and serve in deep plates.

Main courses

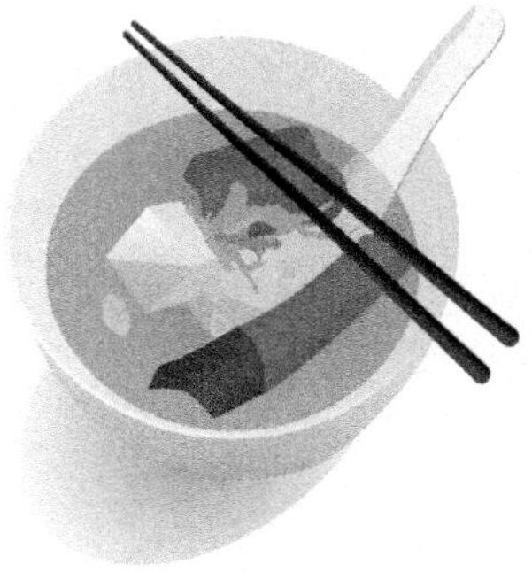

Vegetable - coconut stew

Ingredients (4 people)

200 ml coconut milk

400 g frozen vegetables to taste (carrots, broccoli, etc.)

100 g frozen leaf spinach

300 ml vegetable stock

1 tbsp (rapeseed) oil

2 pinches nutmeg

Salt and pepper to taste

1 tbsp. grated coconut for garnish

Preparation

Bring the vegetable stock to the boil in a large pot and add the frozen vegetables.
Add the oil and nutmeg and simmer for 15 minutes, covered.

Add the coconut milk and bring to the boil briefly.

Season to taste with salt and pepper.

Turn off the heat and let the stew simmer for 5 minutes.

Garnish with grated coconut and serve in deep plates.

Kohlrabi vegetables

Ingredients (4 people)

1 kg kohlrabi

2 carrots

2 potatoes

100 ml cream

1 tsp salt

3 pinches pepper

3 pinches nutmeg

1 tsp vegetable stock

3 tablespoons butter

Boiling water

Preparation

Cut the kohlrabi, potatoes and carrots into cubes.

Cook the vegetables with the salt in a pot of water until soft.

Pour off the water.

Mix with remaining ingredients and Puree.

The kohlrabi vegetables can be served as a side dish, e.g., boiled potatoes.

Borscht

Ingredients (4 people)

400 g white cabbage

400 g beetroot

400 g mainly waxy potatoes

200 g smoked tofu

2 onions

2 garlic cloves

1 tablespoon butter

1 tsp tomato paste

800 ml vegetable stock

200 g pizza tomatoes

1 tsp paprika powder

1 tsp caraway

4 tbsp. cream

2 tablespoons lemon juice

Salt, pepper and vinegar to taste

Preparation

Cut the onions and cabbage into fine strips and press the garlic.

Melt the butter in a large saucepan,

Sauté the onions, cabbage, and garlic for 4 minutes over medium heat.

Add the tomato purée and sauté briefly, stirring.

Pour in stock and tomatoes, season with paprika powder and cumin and cook covered over medium heat for 15 minutes.

Peel the beetroot and potatoes and cut them into 1 cm wide strips.

Add both to the cabbage and cook for another 25 minutes.

Dice the tofu, add and simmer for another 5 minutes.

Season the stew with salt, pepper, lemon juice and vinegar.

Serve with cream.

Falafel

Ingredients

120 g chickpea flour

1 onion, finely diced

2 cloves of garlic, pressed

200 ml water

1 tablespoon parsley

1 tsp salt

½ tsp cumin

½ tsp lemon juice

1 tsp (olive) oil

1 pinch of baking powder

(Olive) oil for frying

Preparation

Bring the water to the boil in a saucepan.

Mix all the dry ingredients together and pour over the boiling water.

Mix well and leave to soak for 15 minutes.

Mix the dough with the lemon juice and oil.

Heat the oil in a pan.

Form falafel with moistened hands and fry over medium heat.

If possible, turn only once and fry covered.

Potato dumplings

Ingredients (4 servings)

800 g potatoes (preferably floury)

200 g potato flour

150 ml lukewarm water

1 tsp salt

Preparation

Boil the potatoes and leave them to cool overnight.

Peel and press through the potato ricer.

Knead with all ingredients to a soft, sticky dough. Add a little more water if necessary.

Shape the potato dumplings and leave them in a pot of boiling salted water for 20 minutes.

The potato dumplings are ready when they float to the top.

Soy Schnitzel "Viennese Style"

Ingredients

Soy Big Steak(s)

Milk

Flour

Breadcrumbs

Salt, pepper and paprika powder

1 lemon cut into wedges

(Rapeseed) oil for frying

Preparation

Soy Big Steaks in boiled salted water for 30 minutes.

Then squeeze the water out of the steaks as well as possible!

Mix the flour, spices, and milk with a whisk, turn the Big Steaks in it, and tap lightly.

Coat the Big Steaks in plenty of breadcrumbs.

Fry the steaks in a pan heated with sufficient oil until golden brown on both sides.

Ready-roasted steaks can be dabbed with some kitchen roll paper.

Serve with lemon wedges and your choice of garnish.

Asian Tempeh Pan

Ingredients (4 people)

400 g tempeh, diced

200 g mushrooms, sliced

200 g sprouts

10 spring onions, sliced

2 carrots, sliced

1 pepper, diced

4 cloves of garlic, finely chopped

2 tsp pepper

2 tsp chilli powder

5 tbsp (rapeseed) oil

5 tablespoons soy sauce and to taste

Side dish: Rice

Preparation

Heat the oil in a large frying pan or wok and fry the tempeh over medium heat for 5 minutes.

Add the mushrooms, peppers and spring onions.

Sauté over medium heat for 5 minutes, stirring frequently.

Add the paprika, garlic cloves, pepper, chilli powder and 5 tbsp. Soy sauce and continue to simmer for 3 minutes, stirring constantly.

Fold in the sprouts and remove the pan from the heat.

Stir in a little soy sauce if desired and serve with rice.

Thai curry

Ingredients (4 people)

100 g brown mushrooms

250 ml vegetable stock

1 carrot

1 pepper

1 onion

40 g peanuts

6 tsp red Thai curry paste

750 ml coconut milk

4 tbsp peanut butter

2 tablespoons honey

7 tbsp (rapeseed) oil

½ tsp ginger

Salt (to taste)

Side dish: Rice

Preparation

Quarter the mushrooms, cut the carrot into fine strips, dice the pepper and cut the onion into strips.

Roast the peanuts in a wok or large frying pan with 1 tbsp oil.

Mix the curry paste with the vegetable stock, ginger powder, coconut milk, peanut butter and honey.

Heat the remaining oil in the wok and sauté the vegetables for 5 minutes.

Add the mixed liquid and bring to the boil.

Leave to infuse on the lowest setting, covered, for 15 minutes.

Season with salt and serve with rice.

Chop Suey

Ingredients (4 people)

2 peppers

150 g cauliflower

100 g broccoli

3 carrots

1 onion

100 g mushrooms

½ jar of soybean sprouts

6 mini - corn on the cob

200 ml water

100 ml soy sauce

2 tablespoons sugar

½ tsp ginger

1 tsp paprika

3 tbsp (sesame) oil for frying

Side dish: Rice

Preparation

Cut the peppers, mushrooms, onion, cauliflower, broccoli, and carrots into bite-sized pieces.

Place the bean sprouts in a sieve and drain well.

Cut the miniature corn cobs in half lengthwise and crosswise.

Bring water to the boil in a saucepan, remove from the heat, add the cauliflower and broccoli and leave to simmer until the sauce is ready.

Bring 150 ml water, soy sauce, sugar, ginger, and paprika powder to the boil in a saucepan.

Dissolve the starch in 50 ml water, then slowly stir it into the sauce.

Bring to the boil briefly, then simmer over low heat until the vegetables are ready.

Heat the oil in a pan.

First, add the carrots; after 2 minutes, add the peppers, mushrooms, cauliflower and broccoli. After another 2 minutes, briefly add the mini corn cobs and bean sprouts and sauté.

Add the sauce and simmer briefly over a low heat (the vegetables should still be firm to the bite).

Serve on warmed plates with rice.

Tip: The vegetable ingredients can be changed at any time. Vegetarian meat substitutes are also delicious.

Chakalaka" vegetable stew

Ingredients (4 people)

1 can of beans baked in tomato sauce

2 carrots

3 peppers

2 onions

3 tsp curry

1 tsp vegetable stock

1 tsp salt

1 tsp pepper

4 tbsp (rapeseed) oil for frying

Side dish: Rice

Preparation

Cut the peppers and carrots into 1 cm cubes. Chop the onion finely.

Heat the oil in a pan and simmer the vegetables for 10 minutes on low heat, stirring frequently.

Add the beans and the rest of the ingredients and simmer on a low heat for another 15 minutes. Stir again and again.

Serve the vegetables with rice.

Potato gratin

Ingredients (2 persons)

500 g potatoes

125 g cream

80 ml milk

150 g grated cheese

A little margarine to grease the casserole dish

Nutmeg

Salt and pepper to taste

Preparation

Preheat the oven to 180° C convection oven.

Grease the casserole dish with a little butter.

Peel and wash the potatoes and cut them into thin slices.

Layer the potato slices in the prepared dish, seasoning each layer with salt, pepper and nutmeg.

Mix the cream with the milk and add.

Spread the grated cheese over the gratin.

Bake in the oven for approx. 45 minutes until the potatoes are soft and the liquid has been absorbed.

Tofu dish "Bibimbap

Ingredients (2 persons)

250 g natural tofu

200 g mushrooms

1 carrot

5 radishes

2 spring onions

½ cucumber

3 handfuls of fresh spinach leaves

1 clove of garlic

2 tablespoons starch

2 tsp soy sauce

5 tbsp. water

2 tbsp (sesame) oil

Chilli paste to taste

Sesame seeds, for sprinkling

Side dish: Rice

Preparation

Grate the cucumber, and carrot, chop the spring onion, press the garlic cloves and slice the mushrooms.

Dry the tofu and cut it into cubes.

Roll the tofu cubes in starch.

Heat the oil in a pan and fry the tofu until crispy.

Deglaze the fried tofu with 1 teaspoon of soy sauce and, after a minute, remove it from the pan and place it on a plate.

Add the mushrooms to the pan and deglaze with soy sauce after frying.

Add water to the pan and sauté the garlic for 2 minutes.

Add the spinach and simmer with the lid on medium heat until the spinach collapses.

Add the remaining ingredients and mix well.

Arrange on a plate, sprinkle with sesame seeds and serve with rice.

Asian vegetables with smoked tofu

Ingredients (4 people)

250 g smoked tofu

2 onions

2 peppers (colour to taste)

1 courgette

2 garlic cloves

1 cm ginger

2 tbsp. soy sauce

1 tbsp rice vinegar (otherwise balsamic vinegar)

1 tsp Asia spice (otherwise season to taste)

2 tbsp (rapeseed) oil

Side dish: Rice

Preparation

Remove the seeds from the peppers, wash and dice them.

Chop the onion and ginger, and press the garlic cloves.

Cut the smoked tofu into small cubes.

Heat the oil in a wok (or large frying pan) and fry the tofu until golden brown and place on a plate.

Sauté the onion, ginger and garlic cloves together in the wok.

Add the peppers and sauté over medium heat for 5 minutes, turning occasionally.

Add the soy sauce, spices and rice vinegar.

Fold in the tofu and fry again briefly over medium heat.

Serve with rice.

Pad Thai" rice noodle dish

Ingredients (2 persons)

250 g rice noodles

100 g natural tofu

2 spring onions

1 onion

1 carrot

1 tomato

2 garlic cloves

4 tbsp coconut milk

3 tbsp. soy sauce

Juice of ½ lime (optional lemon)

2 tbsp chopped peanuts

1 tsp sugar

3 tbsp (rapeseed) oil

Preparation

Finely dice the onion, press the garlic cloves, grate the carrot, dice the tomato and place on a plate.

Dry the tofu well and cut into 1 cm cubes.

Heat 2 tbsp oil in a pan and fry the tofu until golden brown on all sides.

Remove the tofu from the pan and set it aside.

Cut the spring onions into fine rings.

Prepare the rice noodles according to the instructions on the packet.

Heat the remaining oil in a wok or large frying pan.

Add the onions, garlic, carrots, tomatoes and the tofu.

Stir-fry for 4 minutes.

Stir in the coconut milk and continue to cook over a low heat.

When the coconut milk has been combined with the rest, season with soy sauce and sugar.

Turn off the heat completely.

Fold in the rice noodles, drizzle with lime juice and divide between two plates.

Garnish each portion with spring onion rings and chopped peanuts.

Tomato-Lentil Stew

Ingredients

2 cans (400g each) of peeled tomatoes

200 g onions

400 g aubergines

250 g red lentils

3 garlic cloves

1 tbsp cumin

5 tbsp olive oil

1 tsp cinnamon

1 red chilli pepper

1 tsp sugar

500 ml vegetable stock

2 pinches pepper

3 spring onions

5 stalks parsley

1 tsp lemon juice

possibly a little salt

Preparation

Finely chop the onions and garlic.

Heat two tablespoons of olive oil in a large pot.

Sauté the onions and garlic until translucent.

Add the cinnamon, cumin and chilli pepper and steam briefly.

Add a teaspoon of sugar and let it caramelise slightly.

Add vegetable stock and peeled tomatoes and season with pepper.

Reduce the sauce, uncovered, over medium heat for 20 minutes.

Meanwhile, clean the aubergine and cut it into 2 cm thick cubes.

Heat the remaining olive oil in a pan and fry the aubergine on all sides.

Rinse the lentils in a colander and drain.

Add the lentils to the sauce and cook, covered, for 20 minutes.

Add the aubergines 5 minutes before the end of the cooking time.

Clean the spring onions and cut them into fine rings.

Pluck off the parsley leaves and chop coarsely.

Season the stew with salt, pepper, sugar and lemon juice.

Serve with spring onions and parsley.

Mincemeat stew

Ingredients (4 people)

150 g soy granules

2 onions, finely chopped

2 leeks, cut into rings

1000 ml vegetable stock

250 ml cream

5 tbsp tomato paste

1 tablespoon mustard

1 tsp paprika

1 tsp sugar

1 tsp salt

3 pinches pepper

1 tbsp (olive) oil

Side dish: Bread

Preparation

Prepare the soy granules according to the instructions on the packet.

Heat the oil in a pan and fry the onion until translucent.

Add drained soy granules, leek, tomato paste, vegetable stock, mustard and spices.

Simmer for 15 minutes, stirring several times.

Stir in the cream, turn off the heat and leave to infuse for 5 minutes.

Serve on warmed plates and serve with bread.

Ratatouille

Ingredients (4 people)

5 tomatoes, sliced

2 aubergines, diced

1 courgette, diced

3 peppers, diced

2 onions, finely chopped

2 cloves of garlic, pressed

1 tsp thyme

1 tsp parsley

1 tsp basil

2 pinches pepper

1 tbsp (olive) oil

Garnish: baguette or pasta, optional Parmesan cheese

Preparation

Heat the oil in a saucepan and fry the onion and garlic until translucent.

Add the tomatoes, peppers, and spices and saute for 10 minutes on medium heat, stirring occasionally.

Add the aubergines and courgettes and sauté for a further 10 minutes, stirring occasionally.

Serve with a side dish of your choice.

Optionally sprinkle with Parmesan.

Spaghetti Carbonara

Ingredients (4 people)

500 g durum wheat spaghetti

5 litres of water

150 g smoked tofu

1 onion

2 garlic cloves

300 ml milk

4 tbsp (olive) oil

2 pinches pepper

2 tsp salt

1 tsp paprika

2 tsp mustard

4 tbsp parmesan

1 tbsp flour

100 ml cream

Parsley for sprinkling

Preparation

Bring 5 litres of water to boil in a large pot.

Add 1 tsp salt

Simmer the spaghetti on medium heat according to the instructions on the packet (6-8 minutes).

In the meantime, dry and dice the tofu, chop the onion and press the garlic clove.

Heat the oil in a pot.

Fry the onion and garlic until translucent.

Add the smoked tofu and fry over medium heat until crispy.

Mix the Parmesan, flour, salt, paprika and pepper together and stir into the ingredients in the pot.

Add the mustard and briefly sauté all the ingredients, stirring constantly.

Add the milk and bring to the boil.

Mix in the cream, turn off the heat and leave to infuse for 5 minutes.

When the spaghetti is al dente, drain and mix into the sauce.

Season to taste, sprinkle with parsley and serve in deep plates.

Spaghetti Napoli

Ingredients (4 people)

500 g durum wheat spaghetti

2 cans of strained tomatoes

1 onion

2 garlic cloves

1 bunch basil

80 ml (olive) oil

2 pinches pepper

2 tbsp. salt

5 litres of water

Optional Parmesan

Preparation

Bring 5 litres of water to the boil in a large pot.

Add 2 tbsp salt.

Simmer the spaghetti on medium heat according to the instructions on the packet (6-8 minutes).

In the meantime, chop the onions and press the garlic clove.

Heat the oil in a deep frying pan.

Fry the onion and garlic until translucent.

Add the tomatoes and simmer on a medium heat for 10 minutes, stirring.

Add salt, pepper and oil.

Tear the basil leaves into small pieces and mix with the sauce.

When the spaghetti is al dente, drain and mix into the sauce.

Season to taste.

You can use Parmesan cheese as a substitute.

Potato goulash

Ingredients (4 people)

250 g mushrooms

2 potato

1 onion

2 garlic cloves

2 red peppers

2 tsp tomato paste

1 tsp caraway

1 tsp marjoram

1 tsp pepper

1 tsp salt

2 tsp paprika

3 pinches of chilli powder

4 tbsp (rapeseed) oil for frying

Water to cover the potatoes

Preparation

Finely chop the onion, press the garlic cloves, chop the mushrooms, and dice the peppers and potatoes.

Heat 2 tbsp oil in a large saucepan and fry the onion over a medium heat until translucent.

Stir in the tomato purée and after 1 minute, add the potato, pepper and garlic.

After 3 minutes, add enough water to cover the potatoes.

Add the remaining ingredients and simmer for 10 minutes until soft.

If too much water evaporates, add more water if necessary.

Heat the remaining oil in a pan and fry the mushrooms until golden brown.

Stir the mushrooms into the goulash and serve on warmed plates.

Paella

Ingredients (4 people)

200 g basmati rice

500 ml vegetable stock

80 ml white wine

1 onion

2 garlic cloves

2 peppers (colour to taste)

100 g green beans

100 g peas

80 ml (olive) oil

1 tsp paprika powder

1 pinch of chilli powder

1 pinch rosemary

2 pinches cinnamon

1 tsp lemon juice

1 tsp salt

Parsley to decorate. (Olives optional)

Preparation

Press the garlic cloves and chop the onion, beans, and peppers.

Heat the oil in a large frying pan and fry the garlic cloves with the onion and peppers over medium heat for 3 minutes.

Stir in the unwashed rice and sauté for another 2 minutes.

Add the vegetable stock, white wine, lemon juice, and cinnamon and simmer on low for 15 minutes.

Stir in the beans and peas and simmer for another 15 minutes on low heat.

Stir in the salt, chili powder, rosemary, and paprika powder.

Garnish with parsley (and optional olives) on warmed plates.

Mushroom - noodle pan

Ingredients (4 people)

250 g durum wheat spaghetti

1 tsp turmeric

1 onion, diced

3 small courgettes, thinly sliced

250 g mushrooms, sliced

1 tsp cumin

1 tbsp curry powder

4 tbsp. chives or parsley (fresh or frozen)

2 tbsp. soy sauce

(Sesame) oil for frying

Pepper and salt

Preparation

Break (quarter) the spaghetti into four pieces and cook, adding turmeric to the cooking water.

Heat the oil in a pot and sauté the onion.

Add the mushrooms and fry for 3 minutes.

Add the courgettes, cumin, curry powder, and fry for 5 minutes.

Add the spaghetti, soy sauce, pepper, chives/parsley, and mix well.

Pizza

Ingredients (4 people)
400g flour

½ cube yeast

40 ml (rapeseed) oil

200 ml lukewarm water

1 pinch of sugar

1 pinch of salt

Preparation
Dissolve the yeast in the water.

Mix the flour, sugar, and salt.

Add the yeast water to the flour and knead everything until all the flour is bound.

Cover and leave to rise for 20 minutes.

Then knead the dough for 5 minutes.

Shape the pizza dough into a ball and let it rise, covered, for one hour.

Preheat the oven to 180 degrees C convection.

Place the dough on a baking tray lined with baking paper.

Use your hands to carefully form a pizza from the centre to the edges.

Top as desired (such as spread with tomato paste, grated cheese, peppers, tomatoes, mushrooms, etc.)

Bake in the oven for 25 minutes.

Stuffed mushrooms

Ingredients (4 servings)

250 g mushrooms

80 g grated cheese

150 g cream cheese

1 onion

1 pepper

2 tbsp (olive) oil

Paprika powder

Pinch of pepper

½ tsp salt

Preparation

Preheat the oven to a 180° C convection oven.

Line a baking tray with baking paper.

 Peel the onion and cut it into small pieces. Dice the pepper.

Clean the mushrooms and cut out the insides.

Heat the oil in a pan and sauté the inside of the mushrooms.

Add the cream cheese, paprika, onion, paprika powder, pepper, and salt.

Fill this mixture into the mushrooms and cover with the grated cheese.

Place the mushrooms on a baking tray lined with baking paper.

Bake in the oven for 15 - 20 minutes.

Smoked Tofu Casserole

Ingredients

200 g smoked tofu

400 tomato pieces (from the can)

50 ml cream

2 onions. diced

3 cloves of garlic, pressed

2 peppers, cut into cubes

1 aubergine, cut into cubes

1 tbsp (rapeseed) oil

1 tsp oregano

Salt and pepper

Preparation

Preheat the oven to 180 degrees C convection.

Heat the oil in a pan and sauté the onion and garlic until translucent.

Add the paprika and steam for 8 minutes over gentle heat.

Put the warm vegetable mixture together with the tofu and aubergine cubes in a shallow baking dish and mix.

Mix the tomatoes with the cream and season with pepper, salt and oregano.

Pour over the casserole and leave to braise in the oven for about 45 minutes.

Oven vegetables

Ingredients

4 potatoes

1 courgette

2 peppers

2 onions

4 tbsp olive oil

1 - 2 tbsp. spices to taste (rosemary, thyme, oregano...)

Salt and pepper to taste

Preparation

Preheat the oven to 180° C convection oven.

Cut the potatoes into wedges. Cut the courgettes into slices. Cut the peppers into strips. Cut onion into rings.

Line a baking tray with baking paper and spread the vegetables evenly.

Sprinkle the spices over the vegetables.

Cook in the oven for 30 - 35 minutes.

Leave to cool briefly and serve.

Spinach - Risotto

Ingredients (4 people)

300 g risotto rice

400 g fresh baby spinach, cut (or frozen spinach, drained)

1 red chilli pepper, deseeded and finely chopped

2 stalks of lemongrass, make a knot from each stalk.

1 onion, chopped

2 cloves of garlic, pressed

1200 ml vegetable stock

300 ml white wine

1 tablespoon lemon juice

some salt and pepper

2 tbsp (olive) oil

Preparation

Heat the oil in a pot and sauté the onion and garlic.
Add the rice and stir well.

After 1 minute, add white wine and simmer.

Add the lemongrass knots, then gradually add the vegetable stock and cook the risotto for 15 minutes, stirring constantly.

Remove the lemongrass and add the spinach leaves.

Simmer for a further 5 minutes, stirring constantly. (Until the spinach has collapsed).

Season with lemon juice, salt and pepper.

Sweet potato casserole

Ingredients (4 people)

800 g sweet potatoes

400 g chopped tomatoes

250 g strained tomatoes

2 onions

1 clove of garlic

2 tbsp chopped peanuts

1 tbsp peanut butter

1 tsp chilli powder

3 pinches salt

2 tbsp (peanut) oil for frying

Side dish: Rice

Preparation
Preheat the oven to 180 degrees C convection.

Slice the onions, dice the sweet potatoes and press the garlic clove.

Sauté together in a pot heated with oil for 10 minutes over medium heat.

Add tomatoes with spices, and simmer for another 5 minutes.

Add the peanut butter and place it in a baking dish.

Sprinkle with peanuts and bake in a baking dish in the oven for 30 minutes.

Pumpkin ragout

Ingredients

½ Hokkaido pumpkin

250 ml milk

2 tbsp flour

1 tbsp parmesan

1 pinch nutmeg

2 tbsp (rapeseed) oil

Salt

Preparation

Cut the washed and cored pumpkin into pieces of about 2x2 centimetres.

Heat the oil in a saucepan and sauté the pumpkin.

Stir in the flour until it has combined with the oil.

Slowly add the milk. Stir diligently so that no lumps form.

Add the Parmesan and season with salt and nutmeg.

Simmer on low for 15 minutes, occasionally stirring, until the pumpkin cubes are soft.

Kidney Beans - Stew

Ingredients (4 people)

1 tin kidney beans

2 onions

5 Tomatoes

3 garlic cloves

1 tbsp peanut butter

2 tsp sambal oelek

1 tsp cumin

Pinch of salt

(Rapeseed) oil for frying

Parsley for sprinkling

Side dish: Rice

Preparation

Drain the kidney beans and wash thoroughly.

Finely dice the onion and press the garlic cloves.

Cut the tomatoes into cubes.

Heat the oil in a saucepan and sauté the onions until translucent.

Add the tomatoes and simmer for 5 minutes over medium heat.

Add the garlic, salt, sambal oelek, kidney beans and cumin.

Add the peanut butter and bring it to the boil briefly.

Simmer over medium heat for 3 minutes.

Serve with rice and sprinkle with a little parsley.

Nasi Goreng

Ingredients (4 people)

300 g rice

200 g peas (frozen or fresh)

Water for cooking rice and peas

50 g cashew nuts

2 red peppers

1 yellow pepper

1 onion

1 clove of garlic

2 tbsp. soy sauce

1 tsp curry

5 tbsp olive oil

Chilli powder to taste

Preparation

Roast the cashews in a pan without fat and set aside.

Prepare the rice according to the instructions.

Cook the peas in boiling salted water for 8 minutes until tender, and drain.

Cut the pepper into cubes, cut the onion into strips and press the garlic clove.

Heat 3 tbsp olive oil in a pan and fry the rice for 7 minutes.

Sprinkle curry powder over the top and mix well.

Heat the remaining olive oil in a second pan and sauté the onion for 3 minutes.

Add the diced peppers and sauté for another 5 minutes.

Add the garlic and peas to the pan, season with a little chilli powder, and leave to infuse for a while.

Mix the curry rice and vegetables and season with soy sauce.

Serve in a nice bowl and sprinkle with the cashews.

White bean stew

Ingredients (4 people)

250 g white beans (from a can, drained and washed, or dry beans, soaked overnight)

500 ml water

1 tomato

1 pepper

1 carrot

1 onion

1 clove of garlic

2 tsp mint

1 tsp savory

1 tsp salt

1 tsp pepper

1 pinch of bicarbonate of soda

2 tbsp flour

1 tbsp paprika powder

4 tbsp (rapeseed) oil for frying

Side dish: White bread

Preparation

In a pot, boil the beans with water.

Add the baking soda and simmer the beans for 1 hour until soft.

Chop the onion, dice the carrot and pepper, dice the tomato and press the garlic clove.

When the beans are nice and soft but still have the onion, garlic, carrot, and pepper and cook for 10 minutes.

Add the tomato and salt and cook for another 5 minutes.

Add the spices, except for the paprika powder, and let the soup simmer.

In a second saucepan, heat the oil with the flour. Stir constantly with a whisk.

Add the paprika powder and continue to stir until there are no more lumps.

Deglaze with a ladle of the soup and stir.

Add the contents of the second pot to the first pot.

Bring the soup pot to boil again.

Serve with white bread.

Chili sin Carne

Ingredients (4 people)

120 g soy granules

500 ml vegetable stock

400 g chopped tomatoes

1 tin kidney beans (drained weight 240g)

1 pepper

1 can corn

1 onion

2 garlic cloves

2 tbsp tomato paste

1 tsp chilli powder

3 pinches salt

3 pinches pepper

1 piece vegan dark chocolate

Optional 100g cream

2 tbsp (rapeseed) oil for frying

Side dish: Tortilla chips

Preparation

Steep the soy granules in hot vegetable stock.

Drain the soy granules and leave to drain. Collect the cooking liquid.

Cut the onion into small cubes, remove the seeds from the pepper and dice, press the garlic clove, and drain the kidney beans and maize.

Heat the oil in a large pot.

Sauté the soy granules, onion and pepper for 5 minutes over medium heat.

Add the tomatoes, tomato paste, garlic, chilli powder, salt, and pepper and simmer for 15 minutes over medium heat.

Add the kidney beans, corn and chocolate, simmer for another 5 minutes.

If necessary, add the cooking liquid to the chilli and bring it to boil again.

Stir in the optional cream, bring to boil and simmer for 3 minutes at low heat.

Serve with tortilla chips.

The chilli tastes best when it has been infused for a day and then reheated.

Tofu noodles

Ingredients (4 people)

300 g vegan Asian noodles + water for cooking

400 g natural tofu

2 tbsp cornflour

1 onion

2 peppers

1 can corn

400 g Chinese cabbage

1 tsp salt

3 tbsp (peanut) oil for frying

Sauce:

6 tbsp. soy sauce

6 tbsp rice wine

4 tablespoons honey

2 tbsp cornflour

1 tsp ginger

2 garlic cloves

400 ml water

Preparation

Pat the tofu dry as well as possible with kitchen paper. Cut into cubes and place in a freezer bag.

Add 2 tbsp cornflour and shake well to incorporate.

Cook the Asian noodles according to the instructions and drain.

Heat 1 tbsp oil in a pan and fry the tofu cubes for 5 minutes, turning carefully, until golden brown.

Put the tofu cubes aside on a plate.

Squeeze the garlic cloves and mix with all the sauce ingredients in a bowl.

Dice the peppers, and drain the corn. Cut the Chinese cabbage into bite-sized strips.

Heat the remaining oil in a wok or large frying pan.

Sauté the peppers and corn for 5 minutes over medium heat.

Add the Chinese cabbage and stir-fry for another 3 minutes.

Add the soy sauce and simmer, constantly stirring, until the sauce has thickened.

Add the noodles and tofu and heat everything for 2 minutes over a medium heat.

Vegetables - Sushi

Ingredients (4 people)

250 g sushi rice

8 Nori leaves

1 pepper

1 avocado

2 tbsp rice wine

1 tablespoon sugar

Water to coat

Soy sauce for the sushi, wasabi optional

Preparation

Rinse the rice well and bring to boil in a pot covered with water,

Simmer on the lowest heat for 20 minutes.

Put the rice in a bowl.

Stir in the sugar and rice vinegar and leave to cool.

Place a nori sheet, shiny side down, on a rolling bamboo mat and spread a thin layer of rice on top.

Leave 3 cm free at the top and brush the nori sheet with water before rolling it up.

Roll up the nori sheet. This requires some practice. For the first attempts, I recommend watching YouTube videos here.

Place in the fridge until just before serving.

Cut the nori leaf into 3 cm long pieces with a sharp knife.

Serve with soy sauce (and optionally with wasabi).

Spaghetti with peanut sauce

Ingredients

300 g spaghetti

800 ml vegetable stock

120 g roasted peanuts

1 pepper, finely diced

1 carrot, finely diced

3 onions, finely chopped

3 cloves of garlic, pressed

1 piece ginger

1 tablespoon sugar

2 tablespoons lemon juice

2 tbsp peanut butter

1 tsp coriander

1 tbsp. soy sauce

2 tbsp (olive) oil for frying

Preparation
Heat the oil in a saucepan and fry the onion and garlic until translucent.
Add all ingredients except lemon juice and coriander and simmer until the spaghetti is al dente.

Add the coriander and lemon juice. Mix well again and serve.

Coconut spaghetti

Ingredients (4 servings)

500 g spaghetti

600 ml coconut milk

700 ml vegetable stock

4 peppers

4 carrots

2 onions

2 tbsp curry

Pepper and salt to taste

Preparation

Cut the peppers and carrots into small cubes.

Put all the ingredients, except the spaghetti, in a saucepan and bring to boil.

Simmer on a medium heat for 5 minutes.

Add the spaghetti and cook according to the instructions on the packet until al dente.

Season to taste with salt and pepper.

Baked Beans

Ingredients

2 cans of white beans

400 g strained tomatoes

3 tbsp tomato paste

1 onion

1 clove of garlic

3 tablespoons sugar

1 tbsp (rapeseed) oil

Salt

Pepper

Chilli powder

Preparation

Preheat the oven to 180° C convection oven.

Press the garlic clove and chop the onion.

Heat the oil in a pan and fry the onion and garlic until translucent.

Place the beans with the strained tomatoes in a casserole dish.

Add the sautéed onion with the garlic and the remaining ingredients to the casserole dish and mix everything well.

Bake in the oven for 30 minutes.

Pichelsteiner

Ingredients

40 g soy cubes (dry product)

400 g potato, sliced

200 g kohlrabi, sliced

200 g carrots, sliced

200 g celery, sliced or diced

1 leek, in rings

1 onion, chopped

3 tbsp (rapeseed) oil

1000 ml vegetable stock

Salt, pepper and nutmeg

4 tbsp parsley to garnish

Preparation

Bring the soy cubes to boil in the vegetable stock and leave to infuse for 10 minutes. Remove the soy cubes from the vegetable broth with a sieve. Set aside the vegetable stock.

Heat the oil in a pot and add the onion, leek, potato, kohlrabi, celery, carrots and soy cubes in layers.

Season each layer lightly with salt, pepper and nutmeg.

Pour over vegetable stock until the vegetables are ¾ covered.

Cover and simmer for 30 minutes over medium heat. Do not stir! When the potatoes are firm to the bite, stir and serve garnished with parsley.

Spiced rice

Ingredients (4 servings)
350 g basmati rice

1 tsp chilli

1 tsp ginger

1 tsp cinnamon

1 tsp cardamom

1 tsp coriander

1 tablespoon parsley

½ tsp cumin

800 ml water

3 pinches salt

4 tbsp (rapeseed) oil for frying

Preparation
Heat 2 tbsp oil in a saucepan and add the washed rice.

Stir-fry the rice until translucent.

Add all the ingredients except the remaining oil and the parsley.

Bring to the boil and then simmer on the lowest heat for 20 minutes, covered.

Remove the lid from the pot and turn off the stove.

After 2 minutes, stir in the oil and parsley.

Serve in warm plates.

Tofu - Gyros

Ingredients (4 people)

400 g natural tofu

2 tbsp gyros spice

6 tbsp (rapeseed) oil

1 onion

1 clove of garlic

1 tbsp. soy sauce

Side dishes: rice, tzatziki

Preparation

Cut the tofu into 5 mm thick strips.

Carefully marinate with 4 tbsp oil and gyros spice.

Leave to infuse in the refrigerator for at least 1 hour.

Finely press the garlic clove, peel the onion and cut into thin strips.

Heat the remaining oil in a pan and fry the tofu in it.

Add the onion and garlic and fry on high heat until the tofu browns.

Deglaze with soy sauce and season to taste if necessary.

Serve with rice and tzatziki.

Chickpea curry

Ingredients (4 people)

1 tin chickpeas (400 g)

1 can coconut milk (400 ml)

100 ml white wine

1 onion, finely chopped

2 cloves of garlic, pressed

2 tablespoons parmesan

2 tbsp curry

1 tbsp. soy sauce

1 tsp sugar

3 tbsp (rapeseed) oil

Side dish: Rice

Preparation

Heat the oil in a pot and sauté the onion and garlic until translucent.

Deglaze with white wine and simmer a little.

Slowly stir in the coconut milk.

Add the curry, Parmesan, soy sauce, sugar and chickpeas.

Simmer on medium heat for 10 minutes.

Serve the chickpea curry with rice.

Potato - Carrot Rösti

Ingredients (8 Rösti)

200 g potatoes

200 g carrots

2 tablespoons milk

1 tablespoon cornflour

½ tsp lemon juice

Pinch of nutmeg

3 tbsp (rapeseed) oil

Salt

Preparation

Peel the potatoes and carrots and grate them coarsely with a kitchen grater.

Mix with milk, cornflour, lemon juice, salt and nutmeg.

Heat the oil in a pan.

Using round cutters, form 8 equally sized rösti in the pan.

Remove the cutters and allow the rösti to fry on both sides until nice and golden brown.

Paprika - Couscous

Ingredients (4 people)

300 ml vegetable stock

200g couscous

2 peppers

1 tablespoon tomato paste

2 tbsp. soy sauce

2 tbsp curry paste (red or yellow)

2 tbsp white wine vinegar

2 tbsp (olive) oil

Salt, pepper, chilli

Preparation

Heat the curry paste with the vegetable stock in a saucepan and bring to boil.

Add the couscous and remove the pot from the cooker.

Allow the couscous to swell.

Wash, seed and dice the peppers and add to the couscous later.

Stir together the tomato paste, soy sauce and vinegar and add to the couscous and pepper mixture.

Add salt, pepper and chilli and season to taste.

Grilled Pepper skewers

Ingredients

1 each of red, yellow, orange and green peppers.

10 rosemary sprigs

1 tbsp garlic powder

2 tablespoons honey

250 ml olive oil

Salt and pepper

Preparation

Cut the peppers into bite-sized pieces and stick them on the rosemary sprigs.

Mix the olive oil, honey, salt, pepper, and garlic powder and marinate the pepper skewers for 30 minutes.

Preheat the grill and brush the grate with oil.

Grill the pepper skewers for approx. 12 minutes, turning regularly.

Grilled Mushroom Skewers

Ingredients

500 g cleaned mushrooms

4 cloves of pressed garlic

4 tbsp. soy sauce

2 tablespoons honey

1 tsp oregano

1 tsp thyme

2 tbsp olive oil

½ tsp pepper

Preparation

Preheat the grill and brush the grate with oil.

Mix the garlic with the oil, soy sauce, pepper, honey, oregano and thyme to make a marinade. Add the mushrooms to the marinade. Distribute the mushrooms on skewers and place them on the grill. Grill until done, turning regularly.

Grilled corn on the cob

Ingredients

4 corn on the cob

50 g butter

1 tablespoon herb mixture to taste

Some (rapeseed) oil

Preparation

Pre-cook the corn on the cob for about 15 minutes and leave to cool slightly.

Preheat the grill and brush the grate with oil.

Pierce the corn on the cob lengthwise with a barbecue skewer, brush with a little butter, and season with herb mix.

Place the corn on the cobs on the grill and grill evenly for about 10 minutes.

Sauces, dips, dressings and spreads

Guacamole

Ingredients

2 avocado

Juice from one lime

2 garlic cloves

3 pinches of chilli powder

2 pinches salt

1 tsp pepper

Preparation

Halve, pit and peel the avocados.

Blend all ingredients and puree finely.

Raspberry dressing

Ingredients

500 g yoghurt nature

100 g raspberries

1 tbsp (raspberry) vinegar

2 tsp sugar

Preparation

Puree all ingredients with a hand blender or in a blender.

Keep cool.

This dressing goes very well with a mixed salad.

Muhammara

Ingredients

200 g walnuts

5 slices rusk

3 red peppers

2 garlic cloves

6 tbsp olive oil

2 tbsp harissa (or sambal olek)

1 pinch salt

Preparation

Quarter the peppers and put them in a bowl with all the ingredients.

Blend with a hand blender or in a blender to a creamy paste.

Place in a small bowl.

The paprika paste will keep for at least 2 days in the fridge; you can also freeze it.

Sate sauce

Ingredients (4 servings)

300 ml coconut milk

100 g peanut butter

2 onions

1 clove of garlic

½ tsp ginger

½ tsp chilli

½ tsp lemongrass

3 tbsp. lemon juice

1 tsp sugar

1 tbsp. soy sauce

½ tsp salt

1 tbsp (rapeseed) oil

½ tsp coriander

Side dish: Rice (optional vegetables)

Preparation

Chop the onion very finely. Squeeze the garlic clove.

Heat the oil in a pot.

Add the onion, garlic, spices and 3 tbsp coconut milk and sauté for 5 minutes over medium heat.

Add the remaining coconut milk and bring to the boil.

Add the peanut butter and simmer over medium heat, stirring, until a creamy sauce is formed.

Serve on warmed plates over rice and/or vegetables.

Pineapple curry sauce

Ingredients

1 can of pineapple, complete with juice (560g)

1 onion

2 tsp vegetable stock

1 tsp curry

2 pinches chilli

1 tbsp. soy sauce

½ tsp paprika powder

1 tablespoon starch

2 tbsp coconut milk

2 tbsp (coconut) oil

Side dish: Rice

Preparation

Chop the onion finely.

Heat the oil in a pan and fry the onion until translucent.

Add remaining ingredients except for coconut milk and simmer on medium heat for 15 minutes.

Stir in the coconut milk and serve with rice.

Peanut butter

Ingredients

400 g roasted peanuts (unsalted)

30 ml milk

½ tsp salt

Preparation

Blend all ingredients in a blender until creamy.

The peanut butter lasts up to 14 days in the fridge

Hummus

Ingredients

300 g dry chickpeas

300 g sesame paste (tahini)

100 ml oil

Juice of 4 lemons

4 garlic cloves

2 pinches salt

1 tsp pepper

1 tsp paprika powder

1 tsp cumin

Preparation

Soak the chickpeas overnight.

Drain the next day and cook until soft.

Do not pour off the water.

Puree the chickpeas with a hand blender.

Add the sesame paste and blend again.

Add the garlic, spices and lemon juice.

Place the hummus on a deep plate.

Heat the oil and spread it over the hummus.

Coconut spread

Ingredients

250 ml milk

100 g grated coconut

50 ml cream

100 g (coconut blossom) sugar

2 packets of vanilla sugar

Preparation

Stir together everything except the coconut flakes.

Heat the mixture in a saucepan and leave to thicken for an hour over low heat.

Fold in the grated coconut and leave to cool.

The spread will keep in the fridge for up to a week.

Paprika chickpea spread

Ingredients

2 red peppers

3 tsp canned chickpeas

2 tsp sunflower seeds

1 clove of garlic

1 tbsp peanut butter

1 tablespoon olive oil

Salt and pepper (to taste)

Preparation

Deseed and dice the peppers press the garlic clove.

Simmer in a hot pan with oil, paprika and garlic until the mixture thickens.

Mix with remaining ingredients and blend together.

Season the spread with salt and pepper.

Strawberry cream cheese spread

Ingredients

12 strawberries

200 g cream cheese (double cream)

2 tsp honey

1 tsp chilli flakes

Preparation

Wash the strawberries and puree with a hand blender.

Mix with the remaining ingredients.

Spread tastes especially delicious on toasted bread/toast.

Onion lard

Ingredients

200 g coconut oil

1 onion

3 tbsp chopped hazelnuts

1 small apple

½ tsp paprika powder

1 pinch of caraway

1 pinch of pepper

1 tsp salt

Preparation

Chop the onion, peel and core the apple.

Heat the coconut oil in a saucepan and add the onion and sauté.

Briefly steam the remaining ingredients, then remove the pot from the cooker.

Season to taste and leave to cool.

As soon as the mixture sets, whisk well until creamy.

Pour into the desired storage container.

Shelf life: At least 1 week

Hazelnut - Chocolate Cream

Ingredients

400 g roasted hazelnuts

2 tbsp. cocoa

3 tablespoons sugar

1 tbsp rapeseed oil

2 tbsp. cream

½ tsp salt

Preparation

Mix all the ingredients together.

Season to taste and, if necessary, add more sugar and/or cocoa.

Fill the cream into one or more sterile screw jars.

Use up within one week.

Tomato spread

Ingredients

200 g sunflower seeds

50 g dried tomatoes

1 onion, finely chopped

1 clove of garlic, pressed

2 tbsp tomato paste

1 tsp honey

2 tbsp apple juice

5 tbsp olive oil

3 tbsp. lemon juice

3 pinches pepper

2 pinches salt

Preparation

Soak the sunflower seeds in water overnight.

Then bring to the boil and cook for 10 minutes until soft.

Drain the sunflowers.

Heat the oil in a hot pan and sauté the onion and garlic.

Chop the tomatoes, add to the pan with the tomato paste, apple juice, honey, and lemon juice and steam briefly.

Add to the sunflowers and Puree and season with salt and pepper.

Mushroom spread

Ingredients

150 g mushrooms

1 onion

1 tbsp walnut kernels

1 clove of garlic

1 tsp thyme

1 tablespoon parsley

2 tbsp olive oil

3 pinches pepper

2 pinches salt

Preparation

Finely chop the onion and press the garlic clove.

Clean the mushrooms and cut them into small cubes.

Heat the oil in a hot pan and sauté the onion and garlic.

Add the mushrooms to the pan and cook until the water in the mushrooms is gone.

Put all the ingredients in a bowl and blend.

Obatzter

Ingredients

250 g Camembert

1 onion

150 g cream quark

2 tablespoons chive rolls

½ tsp paprika powder

½ tsp pepper

1 pinch of caraway

1 tsp salt

Preparation

Chop the onion finely.

Add the remaining ingredients and puree with a hand blender.

Store in the refrigerator until consumption, within one day.

Vegetarian liver sausage

Ingredients

150 g smoked tofu

200 g chickpeas (tin)

1 onion

2 tablespoons parsley

1 tsp marjoram

1 tsp thyme

1 tablespoon olive oil

½ tsp salt

½ tsp pepper

Preparation

Bring the chickpeas to boil in 1 litre of water and cook on low heat for one hour.

Dice the onion and fry in oil.

Dry the tofu with kitchen paper and dice.

Drain the chickpeas and leave to drain.

Blend all the ingredients together.

Hungarian style paprika sauce

Ingredients

1 red pepper, diced

1 yellow pepper, diced

1 chilli pepper, finely chopped

1 onion, diced

1 clove of garlic, pressed

100 ml vegetable stock

300 ml tomato ketchup

2 tablespoons hot mustard

1 tsp paprika powder

1 tbsp (olive) oil

Salt and pepper to taste

Preparation

Heat the oil in a saucepan and sauté the vegetables.

Stir in the vegetable stock and tomato ketchup.

Return the pan to the cooker and bring it to boil.

Simmer gently over a low heat for 10 minutes, stirring occasionally.

Stir in the mustard and season with salt and pepper.

Aioli

Ingredients

150 ml olive oil

3 cloves of garlic, pressed

1 egg yolk

1 tsp mustard

1 tablespoon lemon juice

1 tsp salt

1 tbsp olive oil for the finish

Preparation

Beat the olive oil and egg yolks with a hand blender to create a creamy mayonnaise.

Stir in the garlic, mustard, lemon juice and salt.

Now slowly add the tablespoon of olive oil.

Leave to infuse in the fridge for 1-2 hours.

The olive oil and egg yolk should be at room temperature for preparation.

Pizza spread

Ingredients

120 g sour cream (or sour cream)

2 tbsp tomato paste

½ red pepper

½ can corn

100 g fresh mushrooms (alternatively from a jar)

1 tsp oregano

150 g grated cheese

Salt and pepper (to taste)

Preparation

Rinse the maize well in a sieve and drain.

Clean the peppers and mushrooms and cut them into small cubes.

Mix together the sour cream, tomato paste and oregano.

Now mix all the ingredients together and season with salt and pepper.

Store in the refrigerator until ready to use.

Tzatziki

Ingredients

500 g yoghurt nature

1 cucumber

2 garlic cloves

2 tablespoons dill

1 tbsp (olive) oil

1 tsp lemon juice

1 tsp salt

1 tsp pepper

Optional 2 tsp ground psyllium husks

Preparation

Press the garlic cloves.

Halve the cucumber, remove the seeds and grate coarsely.

Mix all ingredients in a bowl and leave to infuse for 3 hours.

If you like the tzatziki firmer, you can add 2 tsp of ground psyllium husks when mixing.

Tip: You can also replace the cucumber with 4 gherkins.

Spaghetti sauce "Aglio Olio

Ingredients

200 g young spinach leaves (if frozen, drain)

3 garlic cloves

6 tbsp olive oil

1 tsp chilli flakes

½ tsp salt

Side dish: Italian durum wheat pasta (suggestion: linguine)

Preparation

Press the garlic cloves.

Heat the oil in a large frying pan and sauté the garlic over medium heat.

Add the spinach, chilli flakes, salt, and steam until the spinach has collapsed.

Stir in the cooked pasta and serve on warmed plates.

Pesto

Ingredients

50 g pine nuts

50 g walnut kernels

40 g basil

½ tsp salt

4 tbsp olive oil.

2 tbsp parmesan

Optional: 1 clove of garlic

Side dish: Italian durum wheat pasta

Preparation

Place the pine nuts and walnuts in a heated pan and sauté for 2 minutes, turning frequently.

Place the seeds in a bowl with all the ingredients and blend them to a fine paste.

Pour the pesto over well-drained, still hot pasta.

Lentil spread

Ingredients

500 g red lentils

1000 ml water

100 ml (rapeseed) oil

1 onion

3 garlic cloves

2 tsp turmeric

1 tsp lemongrass

1 tsp coriander

1 tsp pepper

1 tsp cumin

1 tsp chilli powder

1 tsp curry powder

½ ginger

½ tsp salt

Preparation

Chop the onion and press the garlic cloves.

Heat the oil in a pan.

Fry the onion and garlic until translucent.

Add the spices and lentils and fry over medium heat until the lentils are well coated with oil.

Add water, bring to boil and simmer over low heat until the lentils start to break down.

Blend with a hand blender and leave to cool.

This spread lasts 4 days in the fridge and can also be frozen.

Blueberry sauce

Ingredients (4 servings)

200 g blueberries (also called blueberries)

260 ml water

70 g sugar

1 sachet of vanilla sugar

1 tablespoon cornflour

1 pinch of salt

Preparation

Bring the blueberries, 200 ml water, sugar, salt and vanilla sugar to the boil in a saucepan.

Desserts and sweets

Crêpes

Ingredients (8 crêpes)

250 ml milk

250 g flour

1 sachet of vanilla sugar

250 g mineral water

1 tablespoon honey

1 pinch of salt

2 tbsp (rapeseed) oil for frying

Preparation

Mix all ingredients with a whisk to a slightly liquid batter.

Leave the dough covered for at least one hour.

Brush a pan with oil and heat.

Pour half a ladle of batter into the pan.

Swirl the pan and spread the batter evenly.

Bake the crêpes until golden brown.

Fill or top as desired.

Chocolate ice cream

Ingredients

1 can (400 g) coconut milk with 60 % fat

120 ml water

100 g sugar

60 g cocoa powder

Preparation

Bring the water, sugar and cocoa powder to boil in a saucepan, constantly stirring with a whisk.

After boiling, remove the pot from the cooker and leave it to cool for 10 minutes.

Stir in the coconut milk and fill it into a Zippobag. Squeeze out the air and seal.

Place in the freezer for 5 hours.

Allow defrosting for 5 minutes.

In the Zippobag, already break the ice to fit into the blender.

Mix ice.

Ice cream that is not eaten immediately can be frozen in a freezer container.

Waffles

Ingredients (8 waffles)

250 g flour

200 ml milk

120 g butter

70 g cane sugar

3 eggs

2 tsp baking powder

1 sachet of vanilla sugar

Oil to grease the waffle iron

1 pinch of salt

Preparation

Cream the butter and sugar.

Stir in the eggs one by one.

Mix flour with vanilla sugar, salt and baking powder and stir alternately with the milk.

Grease the waffle iron with oil.

Place 2-3 tbsp of waffle batter in the centre of the waffle iron for one waffle.

Bake the batter in the waffle iron until golden brown.

Leave the finished waffles to cool on a cooling rack.

Top/sprinkle waffles as desired.

Sweet couscous

Ingredients (4 servings)

400 g couscous, prepared according to the package instructions

8 dates (pitted)

1 pomegranate

5 tbsp sultanas

Hot water for swelling the sultanas

4 tbsp flaked almonds

3 tablespoons butter

3 tbsp. orange juice

4 tsp cinnamon

2 tablespoons honey

1 pinch of salt

4 tbsp icing sugar for garnish

Preparation

Put the sultanas in a bowl, pour hot water over them, and leave to soak.

Remove the red fruit seeds from the pomegranate and cut the dates into eighths.

Toast the flaked almonds in a pan without fat until light brown.

Stir the butter into the finished couscous.

Drain the sultanas and leave them to drain.

Mix all the ingredients, except the icing sugar, with the couscous.

Portion onto small, warmed bowls and serve dusted with icing sugar.

Lemon - Donuts

Ingredients (12 donuts)

200 g flour

250 ml milk (recommendation: almond drink)

150 g apple syrup (also called apple sweetener)

120 g grated almonds

80 g icing sugar

2 tablespoons butter

5 tbsp. apple puree

1 sachet of vanilla sugar

1/2 tsp baking powder

1 pinch of bicarbonate of soda

2 organic lemons

1 pinch of salt

100 ml (rapeseed) oil for frying

Preparation

Preheat the oven to 180 degrees C convection.

Grease 12 - 16 donut moulds (number depending on the size of the moulds) with butter and place them on a baking tray.

Grate the lemon zest and squeeze out the juice.

Mix together the flour, almonds, baking soda, salt, and baking powder in a bowl.

In a second bowl, mix together the applesauce, apple syrup, vanilla sugar, oil, almond milk, half of the lemon zest, and a good half of the lemon juice.

Slowly stir the contents of the second bowl into the first bowl.

Divide the batter into the donut moulds and bake for 25 minutes.

Mix the icing sugar with the remaining lemon juice and lemon zest and brush over the cooled donuts.

Pancake

Ingredients (8 pancakes)

200 ml milk

200 g flour

2 eggs

50 g sugar

50 g oil

1 tsp baking powder

1 pinch of salt

some (rapeseed) oil or butter for frying

Preparation

Mix the flour, baking powder, salt, oil, milk, eggs and sugar in a bowl with a whisk until smooth.

Melt the butter in a pan and stir into the batter.

Warm a tsp of oil in a pan (not hot!), then pour the batter into the pan using a small ladle.

Fry the pancakes for 2 minutes, turn over and fry again for 1 minute.

Add a little oil again before the next pancake.

Spread or top finished pancakes as desired.

Apple-almond porridge

Ingredients

2 apples

150 g oat flakes

100 g ground almonds

600 ml milk

1 pinch cinnamon

Honey

Preparation

Briefly bring the milk to boil in the cooker

Over medium heat, add the oat flakes, cinnamon and ground almonds.

Stir into a creamy paste.

Peel the apples, remove the core and cut them into thin slices.

Fill porridge into four muesli bowls and spread apple slices on top.

Chia pudding

Ingredients

20 g chia seeds

80 ml milk

300 g yoghurt

about 50 g of fresh or frozen berries

2 tablespoons honey

1 tbsp roasted sunflower seeds

Preparation

Put the chia seeds in a bowl, add the milk and cover with cling film.

Place in the refrigerator overnight. The chia seeds soak up the milk and become about four times the size they were before.

In the morning, add thawed or fresh berries or cut fruit with yoghurt and mix with a little honey to sweeten.

Sprinkle with roasted sunflower seeds as a topping.

Pancakes

Ingredients (4 pancakes)
250 ml milk

200 g wheat flour

2 eggs

50 g icing sugar

1 sachet of baking powder

50 g butter

1 pinch of salt

3 tbsp (rapeseed) oil for frying

Preparation
Mix the flour, icing sugar, baking powder and salt in a bowl and make a well in the centre.

Pour the milk and eggs into the well and mix with a hand mixer until a slightly runny mixture forms.

Heat the pan with a little oil (not hot!), then pour the batter into the pan with a ladle.

The batter does not have to cover the whole bottom of the pan like a pancake.

Let the dough continue to bubble on medium heat and watch it slowly firm up from the edge to the centre.

Once the centre is almost firm, turn the pancake.

Wait a good minute and the pancake is ready.

Set aside on a warm plate and make the remaining pancakes.

Baked banana

Ingredients (2 servings)

2 bananas

2 tbsp chia seeds

1 tablespoon honey

1 tbsp breadcrumbs

1 pinch cinnamon

1 pinch of vanilla sugar

(Coconut) oil for frying

Preparation

Cut the peeled bananas in half lengthwise.

Spread the bananas with honey.

Combine remaining ingredients, except oil.

Roll the bananas in the mixture.

Heat the oil in a pan and fry the bananas in it.

Serve the baked bananas garnished with chia seeds.

Banana cookies

Ingredients (12 - 15 cookies)

2 ripe bananas

100 g grated coconut

1 sachet of vanilla sugar

Preparation

Preheat the oven to 180° C convection oven.

Peel and slice the bananas.

Puree the slices in a bowl with the grated coconut and vanilla sugar.

Line a baking tray with baking paper and spread the dough in portions with a tablespoon.

Flatten the portions slightly and shape them a little with the tablespoon.

Bake the cookies for 20 to 25 minutes until lightly browned on the edges.

Brownies

Ingredients

80 g dark chocolate

180 g flour

200 g sugar

50 g cocoa powder

1 sachet of vanilla sugar

1 tsp baking powder

½ tsp cinnamon

100 ml milk

100 ml honey

100 ml rapeseed oil

100 ml apple juice

Preparation

Preheat the oven to 180° C degrees. Line a baking dish with baking paper. Chop the chocolate with a knife.

Mix the flour, sugar, cocoa, vanilla sugar, cinnamon, and baking powder in a bowl.

Mix the milk, honey, oil, and apple juice and pour into the flour mixture.

Mix the dough with the beaters of a hand mixer for 2 minutes at the highest speed. Fold in the chocolate.

Pour the batter into the baking dish and smooth it out.

Bake in the oven for about 40 minutes.

Leave to cool. Cut the brownies into desired pieces.

Schokocrossies

Ingredients

100 g cornflakes

200 g dark chocolate

Preparation

Melt the chocolate in a water bath.

When the chocolate has completely melted, stir in the cornflakes.

Line a baking tray with baking paper.

Place small portions on the baking tray and refrigerate until the chocolate crispies are firm using a teaspoon.

Chocolate muffins

Ingredients

300 g flour

250 g sugar

50 g cocoa powder

1 package of baking powder

7 tbsp rapeseed oil

350 ml water

1 pinch of salt

Muffin - paper cups

Preparation

Preheat the oven to 180° C convection oven.

Mix flour with cocoa powder, baking powder, sugar, salt, oil and water well.

Pour the batter into small muffin paper cups and bake for approx. 30 minutes.

Popcorn with caramel sauce

Ingredients (2 servings)

50 g popcorn corn

40 g butter

40 g sugar

1 tablespoon honey

1 tbsp (rapeseed) oil

70 g cashew nuts (optional)

Preparation

Heat the butter, sugar and honey in a saucepan.

Cook on high heat, constantly stirring, for 2 minutes and then set aside.

(Optional) Toast the cashews in a frying pan on medium heat for 4 minutes, stirring until golden brown. Then place on a plate.

Pop the popcorn corn in the pot with oil according to the instructions. Occasionally shake the pot and hold the lid.

Pour the caramel sauce over the popcorn and cashews and mix well.

Place the popcorn on a baking tray lined with baking paper, spread out and leave to cool.

Serve only when it is well dry.

Dulce de leche" dessert

Ingredients

1 L milk

400 g sugar

200 ml cream

1 sachet of vanilla sugar

Preparation

Put all the ingredients in a pot.

Bring to the boil and simmer at medium heat for 1 to 1½ hours.

The dulce de leche is ready when it is viscous.

Chocolate mousse

Ingredients (4 people)

200 g dark chocolate

1 Egg

1 egg yolk

1 tsp brandy

400 g cream

Preparation

Melt the chocolate in a water bath.

Beat the egg with the egg yolk in a bowl in a hot water bath until foamy.

Whisk in the chocolate and brandy.

Whip the cream until stiff and fold into the lukewarm mousse.

Divide the mousse between bowls and place it in the fridge for an hour.

Strawberry - Tiramisu in a glass

Ingredients

700 g strawberries

150 g biscuits (Amarettini - or chopped ladyfingers)

150 g cream

350 g curd

70 g sugar

some amaretto

Preparation

Cut the strawberries into small pieces.

Pour a little amaretto over the biscuits.

Whip the cream and stir in the quark with sugar.

Place a few biscuits in the glass, then spread a layer of cream on top.

Spread the strawberries over the cream.

Pour some cream over the strawberries and decorate with 1-2 biscuits.

Leave to infuse in the fridge for 2 hours.

Also very tasty with raspberries!

Roasted almonds

Ingredients

200 g almonds

50 ml water

50 g sugar

1 packet of vanilla sugar

1/2 tsp cinnamon

1 pinch of salt

Preparation

In a heated pan, bring water with sugar, vanilla sugar and cinnamon to boil.

Add the almonds and stir frequently. When the sugar starts to become crumbly, continue stirring. The sugar must melt and draw threads.

Place the almonds on a baking tray lined with baking paper and leave to cool. The almonds must lie separately; otherwise they will stick together.

Chocolate cake

Ingredients

For the dough
300 g flour

250 g sugar

5 tbsp cocoa powder

125 g vegan dark chocolate, chopped

1 sachet of baking powder

350 ml milk

4 tablespoons rum

130 ml (rapeseed) oil

2 tsp locust bean gum

For the decoration
150 g vegan dark chocolate
2 tbsp icing sugar

Preparation

Preheat the oven to 180° C convection oven.

For the dough, mix all the dry ingredients in a bowl.

Add the milk, rum and oil and mix with a hand mixer until smooth.

Pour the batter into a springform pan lined with baking paper.

Bake in the oven for 45 minutes.

Apple tart

Ingredients
For the dough

80 g butter, a little more for greasing

250 g sugar

150 g flour, a little more for flouring

50 ml water

1 tsp vanilla sugar

For the topping

1 kg apples

40 g sugar

10 g butter

Preparation

Preheat the oven to 180°C convection oven.

Grease and flour the tart tin (Ø 26cm).

Mix all the dough ingredients in a bowl and knead them into a dough.

Roll out the dough on a lightly floured work surface and line the tart tin with it.

Peel and core the apples, cut them into thin slices and spread like a fan on the pastry.

Sprinkle with sugar and spread the butter on top.

Bake in the oven for 35 minutes.

Strawberry sorbet

Ingredients (4 people)

600 g strawberries, frozen

70 g sugar

300 ml water

2 lemons

Preparation

Squeeze the lemons into a bowl.

Bring the water, sugar and 6 tbsp lemon juice to the boil in a saucepan.

Stir until the sugar has dissolved.

Leave the lemon syrup to cool.

Finely purée the strawberries with the syrup.

Season to taste with the remaining lemon juice.

Place in the freezer for 15 minutes.

Shape the strawberry sorbet with an ice cream scoop and serve.

Red wine cake

Ingredients

200 g margarine

250 g flour

150 g chocolate flakes

125 ml red wine

50 g chopped hazelnuts

4 eggs

200 g sugar

1 sachet of vanilla sugar

1 sachet of baking powder

2 tsp cocoa powder

1 tsp cinnamon

1 tsp rum

Icing sugar for sprinkling

Preparation

Preheat oven to 180° C convection oven. Beat the eggs until frothy.

Add the sugar and vanilla sugar and continue to beat until frothy.

Add the margarine while stirring. Add the remaining ingredients one by one and stir.

Pour the dough into a well-greased loaf tin. Bake in the oven for approx. 40 minutes. Test with a chopstick whether the cake is baked through.

Transfer the cake to a cooling rack and leave to cool.

Sprinkle with icing sugar.

Drinks and smoothies

Banana milkshake

Ingredients

1 ripe banana

250 ml chilled milk

1 tablespoon honey

Optional ½ packet vanilla sugar

Preparation

Put all the ingredients in the blender and blend together for about one minute.

Golden milk

Ingredients (2 glasses)

250 ml milk

1 tbsp turmeric

1 tsp coconut oil

2 pinches ginger

½ tsp cinnamon

1 pinch nutmeg

1 pinch of pepper

Possibly honey (sweeten to your own taste)

Preparation

Mix all the ingredients together.

Heat together in a saucepan, but do not boil.

Mulled wine

Ingredients (6 cups)

1000 ml red wine

1 orange, sliced

2 sticks cinnamon

3 cloves

Sugar to taste

Preparation

Heat all the ingredients in the pot, but do not let them boil.

Mulled wine is best served nice and warm.

Children's punch

Ingredients (6 glasses)

500 ml water

500 ml apple juice

1 litre elderberry juice

4 oranges, sliced

Grated lemon zest of one lemon

1 cinnamon stick

4 cloves

Preparation

Bring the water to the boil in the pot.

Add the lemon zest, cinnamon, and cloves and turn off the heat.

In the second pot, slowly heat the apple and elderberry juices. The juices must not boil! Add the orange slices and turn off the heat.

After about 10 minutes, carefully pour the pots together and leave to infuse for a few hours.

Reheat before serving.

Lemonade

Ingredients

3 large organic lemons

750 g sugar

50 g citric acid

1 litre of hot water

Preparation

Wash the lemons and grate the zest. Squeeze out the lemon juice.

Mix the lemon zest with the sugar, citric acid and the hot water, and leave to cool.

Add the lemon juice. Pour the syrup into a bottle and leave it to infuse for one day in the refrigerator.

To drink, pour the syrup into a glass to approx. 1 cm and top up with cold mineral water.

The syrup can be kept for at least one month.

Strawberry Yoghurt Smoothie

Ingredients

150 g strawberries (fresh or frozen)

250 g natural yoghurt

1 ripe banana

With fresh strawberries, I recommend adding 3 - 4 ice cubes.

Preparation

Puree all the ingredients in a blender or large bowl with a hand blender.

Pour into glasses and serve.

Raspberry Smoothie

Ingredients

200 g raspberries (fresh or frozen)

100 ml water

100 ml milk

1 tsp vanilla sugar

with fresh raspberries, I recommend adding 3-4 ice cubes.

Preparation

Puree all the ingredients in a blender or large bowl with a hand blender.

Pour into glasses and serve.

Of course, you can also use other berries.

Green smoothie

Ingredients (2 servings)

1 ripe banana

1 Apple

300 ml water

150 g baby spinach frozen (add 50 g ice cubes if fresh)

Preparation

Core the apple.

Puree all the ingredients in a blender or large bowl with a hand blender.

Pour into glasses and serve.

This basic recipe can, of course, be modified.

Add raspberries if desired.

A smoothie can also be very thick. You should actually spoon the smoothie like a yoghurt.

Pineapple Smoothie

Ingredients (4 glasses)

200 g pineapple, fresh or canned

500 ml milk

200 g natural yoghurt

2 tablespoons honey

Preparation

Peel and cut the pineapple.

Place the pineapple chunks in a measuring cup.

Add the milk, yoghurt, and honey, mix everything well with a blender, and pour into a large glass.

Strawberry Banana Smoothie

Ingredients (2 glasses)

200 g strawberries

1 ripe banana

200 ml orange juice

Preparation

Wash and clean the strawberries. Put them in a blender.

Peel the bananas, cut them into small pieces, and put them into the blender.

Pour in the orange juice and puree everything finely.

Watermelon Smoothie

Ingredients (2 glasses)

400 g watermelon

Ice cube

Preparation

Divide the watermelon. Cut some off for garnish if needed and cut into pieces.

Peel the rest, remove the seeds and cut them into small pieces. Put the flesh in a blender or food processor and puree until smooth.

Put a few ice cubes in each of the two glasses and pour the smoothie over them. Garnish with the watermelon pieces and serve. It's super thirst-quenching, refreshing and really quick to make.

Kiwi Banana Smoothie

Ingredients (2 glasses)

1 ripe banana

2 ripe kiwis

250 ml milk

1 tbsp lemon juice (preferably freshly squeezed)

Preparation

Puree all ingredients in a blender or large bowl with a hand blender.

Disclaimer

Implementing all information, instructions and strategies contained in this book is at your own risk. The author cannot accept liability for any damages of any kind for any legal reason. Liability claims against the author for material or non-material damage caused by the use or non-use of the information or incorrect and/or incomplete information are fundamentally excluded. Any legal claims and claims for damages are therefore also excluded. This work was compiled and written down with the greatest care and to the best of our knowledge and belief. However, the author accepts no responsibility for the information's topicality, completeness, and quality. Misprints and incorrect information cannot be completely excluded. No legal responsibility or liability of any kind can be accepted for incorrect information provided by the author.

Printed in Great Britain
by Amazon

37740473R00109